Freight Broker & Trucking Business Startup

Step-by-Step Guide to Start, Grow and Run
Your Own Freight Brokerage & Trucking
Company in as Little as 30 Days

Clement Harrison

Table of Contents

Freight Broker Business Startup

Trucking Business Startup

Freight Broker Business Startup

Step-by-Step Guide to Start, Grow and Run Your Own Freight Brokerage Business in as Little as 30 Days

Clement Harrison

Introduction

"A small business is an amazing way to serve and leave an impact on the world you live in."

Nicole Snow

Every morning, we wake up to the news of entrepreneurs making huge strides in the world of business. As much as their success can be attributed to their efforts, have you ever wondered how all these businesses come to thrive? Beyond the technical or professional aspects of their operations, almost all businesses depend on some deliveries. Look at companies like Amazon that have revolutionized the transport and logistics industry. They ship almost anything you can think of under the sun. In a world as interconnected as ours, freight transport and logistics are among the most crucial business entities in the world, responsible for the success stories you read about in the news. Unfortunately, they never get the acclamations.

Take a moment and think of a world without the freight industry. Imagine the challenges we would go through, struggling to get cargo from one point to the other. It's unfathomable. The freight transport industry is vast, and there is enough space for you in it, too. Starting and running a freight brokerage business is not an easy task. For someone new to the industry, it might sound like an insurmountable task. Even those who have worked in the industry for years might not be able to wrap their heads around taking that leap of faith and starting their own brokerage business. This guide will help you to start and run a freight brokerage business.

Regardless of your experience in the industry, the requirements, rules and legal obligations in the industry are clear. Using this book, you are well on your way to learning how to prepare yourself for the business, drawing up a business plan, researching the market and even carving out a niche for yourself.

The job prospects and outlook for freight brokers is exciting today. It is one of the fastest-growing sectors in the transport industry. Online shopping has made it easier for people to purchase virtually anything they want regardless of where it is located and that is one of the reasons for the steady growth in the freight industry. This points to one thing—there is a demand for freight brokers.

Shippers need carriers to move cargo from one point to the next. However, it is difficult for most shippers to coordinate with carriers. This is where you come in. You are the liaison between the shipper and carrier, and in the process, you earn a tidy sum for your effort. Freight brokerage offers you a lot of flexibility and independence such that you can become your own person. You can run the business on your own and bring one or a few more people to assist as your business grows.

You don't even need a physical office to start. Many freight brokers leverage their businesses by working from home and, using some of the best software in the market, coordinate cargo movement with carriers to the shipper's destination. If you are the kind of person who doesn't like someone breathing down their neck, this is something you should think about.

The freight industry has so much potential for growth. I have seen many young entrepreneurs start from scratch and, in a few years, grow their brokerage businesses into large companies, hiring agents to work under them.

The door to personal and business success opens to anyone who is bold enough to pursue their dreams. You have to be passionate about what you set your mind to. By all means, I have enjoyed all manner of success because I took a chance and invested in my financial future. When you don't come from generational wealth, you have to put in the work, at times harder than everyone else. That is the grit that helped me to succeed in life.

Freight brokerage is an incredible business opportunity. One of the reasons I love this particular venture is the kind of people you meet all the time. With all manner of cargo passing through your hands, you rub shoulders with companies and individuals you might never have imagined meeting, but that's beside the point.

My vision while writing this book was to give you the best introduction to the freight brokerage business. I realize that you might be at a different point in life than the next individual, so the challenge was getting everyone on the same page. Whether or not you have experience in the freight industry, you will find this book useful. You will learn, among other things, how to find shippers and carriers, instructions on the brokerage license, marketing techniques to make your brand visible, and how to choose the right business structure within which you will operate the business.

This book is organized so that you can use it as a guide in every step of your brokerage business. You will learn not only how to start the business but also how to find clients. Speaking of clients, one of the common fears I have come across in the freight brokerage industry is that the market is saturated, making it difficult for them to set out on their own. This is nothing but fear of the unknown, which happens to the best of us, and is normal in business. As much as the freight industry is saturated, new customers are coming into the market every other day. The industry has grown over the years, and with growth comes the need for specialization, diversification and other disruptive approaches. You can be a part of this new dynamic. I included an industry forecast to show you how good the prospects are, which is why you need to overcome the defeatist mentality that the market is saturated.

For most entrepreneurs, just getting into the business and facing the reality of writing a business plan is another stumbling block. I realized that many people had never written a business plan, and that is also okay. I mean, you probably never imagined you'd find yourself building a business from scratch, right? You will learn how to write a business plan and the importance of one.

The freight business is a relationship business. You need connections to make it in this industry. Even if you don't know anyone, let your business acumen do the talking for you. Network, join discussion forums, talk to former colleagues, do everything you can to get your business name on people's lips. Build relationships with carriers and shippers, and more importantly, be efficient, and you will run a successful freight brokerage business.

From my experience in this industry, freight brokerage is not for the weak. You must be a passionate, result-driven fellow to cut it in this industry. Your attitude and motivation will be key to your success in freight brokerage.

Chapter 1
A Freight Broker—The World's Most Sought After Middle Man

Logistics is one of the most critical departments in a business and the unsung hero in many success stories. Every other day you see companies posting impressive performance reports at the close of their financial year, and most of these are attributed to their sales and marketing efforts. Take a moment and think about it, where would companies like Amazon be without an efficient logistics network? You can market all you want, spend so much money on advertising, offer promotions, giveaways and all manner of offers to entice customers. But behind the scenes, an inefficient logistics network will render your efforts null and void. I mean, what's the point of promoting your business if you cannot deliver on time, and that's if you deliver at all, right?

Freight brokerage is an essential part of the logistics business. Do I really need to use a freight broker? This is a common question in shipper circles. To answer this question, let's understand what a freight broker does. A freight broker is someone who organizes the smooth movement of consignments between shippers and carriers. For making this movement smooth, they receive a commission. Essentially, without a freight broker, the shipper-carrier engagement is often marred with several inconveniences and mishaps. Freight brokers, therefore, bring a vital element to shippers and carriers—value addition.

Over the years, businesses have grown through specialization—focusing on the things they are good at and outsourcing the rest to experts. By focusing on their core business, entities can leave things like logistics to freight brokers because that is their specialty. Through freight brokers, value addition is realized by increased efficiency and flexibility in moving items through the supply chain from the originator to the end-user. Unless their core business is shipping, many businesses today use freight brokers for shipping and logistics. Here's an interesting fact: More than 80% of Fortune 500 companies use freight brokers and other third-party firms to handle services that are not primarily in their purview.

Looking at this scenario, you must understand your role in the supply chain when you venture out as a freight broker. Customers need value, which you will offer through your experience, expertise and connections in the industry. This is not a coincidence either, because it is essentially a cause-and-effect relationship. The money saved by your clients on shipping improves their business model, helping them scale their operations. As they grow, their business volume under your docket grows, so you grow too.

Freight brokerage is such a close-knit industry that if you don't add value to the customer, they will always look to get better services elsewhere. So, in your capacity, the following are some benefits you must bring to the table or face extinction:

1. **Scalability and flexibility**

As businesses evolve through different cycles, you prop them up through your brokerage services. This way, you offer your business partners less or more capacity as and when their business needs arise. This is important because, among others, you eliminate the challenge of seasonality in some industries.

In the long run, you offer businesses an opportunity to save money, time and other resources, which they can then divert towards strengthening the core functions of their operations. You essentially provide businesses a dedicated shipping and logistics department without them incurring the cost of setting up and running it on their own. In terms of the weight off their shoulders, think of training, auditing, invoices, repair and maintenance, staffing and the associated costs. You are that strategic partner every business needs.

2. **Professionalism**

Business partners come to you for the one thing you are good at—shipping. By all means, make sure you are good at it. By working with you, they leverage their business on your knowledge, experience and grasp the industry's best practices. This, coupled with access to the latest technology in the industry, helps you to offer them the level of service they would appreciate.

One thing you should never take for granted in this industry is networking. The freight brokerage business is one where connections matter more than what you know. From your networks, customers hope to benefit from volume discounts, capacity handling, and any other service that would make working with you better than the prospect of running an internal shipping department.

3. **Partnership**

When you start working with shippers and carriers, you become a strategic partner. This is not a one-off business venture. Since you essentially work for the customers, you must prioritize their needs and interests. Look at it this way, if they succeed, you succeed. If their business grows, yours grows. This is the kind of mutually beneficial partnership that you should strive to achieve.

Role of a Freight Broker

Having seen what you bring to the table, what is your role in this industry? You are the most in-demand middleman in the world of business. Primarily, your work is to help shippers and carriers. You connect shippers with carriers who are qualified and ready to transport their cargo. Once you broker a deal between the shipper and carrier, you facilitate the movement of their load until it gets to the intended destination. This means that you need to keep an open line of communication between the shipper and carrier throughout the process. You might not be a carrier or shipper, but you play an important role in cargo movement as a transport intermediary.

Regardless of the size of your operation, there are some tenets that you must follow if you are to succeed in the industry. As we discuss them below, you will realize that they are all related. Together, they will help you cultivate an environment where your brokerage business can grow and offer shippers and carriers quality services.

1. Ensure freight is insured

One of your responsibilities is to ensure that all cargo you handle has appropriate insurance coverage and that the selected carriers also have relevant liability coverage. When handling cargo, your shipper must disclose the value of the cargo. This helps determine the liability cover value, which is usually determined by factors like the type of commodity, value, class and so on.

2. Carrier selection

This might sound obvious, but it is important to ensure that you offer your customers quality services. There are many carriers in the industry, but not all are always suitable for the task. You must understand the shipper's needs, and where applicable, the specific needs of their cargo; hence, finding an appropriate carrier.

For example, most carriers' average load height is 96". In case your shipper's load is 100", you have to rethink the conventional delivery method. Perhaps a flatbed would be better than a regular truck, to make loading easier, in this case. You could also consider a trailer with swing doors, making it easier to load the cargo. This is why understanding the customer's freight and their needs is important. You can be certain that if you pull this off without a hitch, you will be the go-to broker for that shipper's business. Where possible, advise the shipper on all the options available to them.

3. **Instruct carriers**

One of the common documents you will use is a bill of lading. In this document, you provide all the information necessary about the cargo to the carrier. For example, perhaps the delivery is to a residential area, maybe the shipper expects a call before delivery to make special arrangements, and so on. You must convey all the instructions requested by the shipper to the carrier, even if they seem unorthodox.

Most shippers will be upfront with you if there are special instructions or requests to go with their cargo. It is only fair that you do the same with carriers, so there are no surprises when delivering the cargo.

4. **Check carrier safety ratings**

Always vet carriers, and know their safety and liability ratings. Carriers run into unavoidable problems on the road from time to time, so it is wise to ensure their ratings are within an acceptable score range.

Given the industry's competition, some carriers offer ludicrous prices that are too good to be true. Note that some carriers offer incredibly low prices as they cannot compete with qualified competitors at the same price because of low safety and liability scores. Many freight brokers have fallen prey to the allure of cheap freight, only to suffer losses in the long run. Each time you assign a shipper's cargo to a carrier, your reputation is on the line until the shipment arrives at the intended destination and in the expected condition.

There are many qualified carriers out there, and it is your duty to find them, know their rates and ensure that the shipper's freight arrives safely and efficiently. At the moment, identity theft has crept into the industry, so you must be careful when vetting carriers. Organized crime rings have drivers whose safety ratings check out, but they use fake motor carrier numbers to steal consignments in the real sense. This is also a good reason to ensure your business.

5. **Cost reduction**

Everyone worries about costs when running a business. In particular, shippers are more concerned about costs because it eventually influences the price at which they can conduct business and break even. Cost reduction is one of the reasons why shippers look for freight brokers. Making a profit in any business is about thin margins, and this is where you come in.

Shippers rely on your experience and connections to streamline their supply chain, and in the process, find ways of reducing the logistics costs compared to what they would spend if they moved cargo on their own. Besides, you are a consultant, so the shipper does not need an in-house freight handling department with employees, saving them more money in the process.

Shippers and Carriers

In freight logistics, a carrier is an individual or company with the legal obligation of transporting cargo on water, land or air. Carriers work with shippers to move stuff from one place to the next. There are two types of carriers in the market: contract carriers and common carriers.

Contract carriers refer to the individuals or companies that offer transport services for a shipper, but on a long term arrangement. The contract carrier and the shipper sign a contract whereby they work together for a predetermined period and under specific conditions.

On the other hand, common carriers are individual or company transport providers who offer carrier services to anyone or any company. They must be licensed to offer their services. Since they are not bound by contract to a specific shipper, common carriers can work with as many shippers as they can handle within the day.

Another term that you will come across in the industry is a global freight forwarder. This is a carrier that handles shipments from one country to the other. Some carriers are contractually bound to operate only within the country, offering interstate transport and logistics services.

In terms of the delivery services, carriers offer different modes of transport. As a freight broker, it is always advisable to look for carriers who provide multiple transportation modes. This gives you a lot of options when moving a customer's cargo. Ideally, the decision on how to transport the shipper's cargo usually depends on their express instructions, the costs involved, and the cargo's nature.

There are several authority organizations to which freight carriers should be registered. They oversee operations within the transportation industry and set standard rules of engagement and practices under which cargo is moved. As a freight broker, you should know about the governing bodies in your industry so that, when vetting carriers, you choose only those who are duly licensed. Note that the carrier you choose will be responsible for transporting goods worth millions of dollars for your shipper customers. Therefore, you must exercise due diligence in this regard. Besides, your reputation is on the line, so ensure that you choose carriers who share the same business growth values as you do.

Shippers are individuals or businesses that own or supply the cargo being transported by the carrier. Shippers are also known as consignors.

Freight Broker Duties

One of the realities of life as an intermediary is that your duties are always diverse. Given that you are running the business on your own, for example, you might not be in a position to delegate tasks. Unless you start your brokerage business with a team to help from time to time, all the work involved in the brokerage business is on you. Let's have a look at some of the tasks you will have to do:

Logistics Operations

Well, this is a logistics-based business, so you must be prepared for this. If you have been in the brokerage industry before, you have some knowledge of some of the logistics tasks you will perform. Even if you are new to the industry, a broker's logistics duties are things you can manage and get used to easily. Here are some of your duties:

- Coordinating and planning delivery and pick-up schedules between carriers and shippers

- Managing dispatch schedules

- Monitoring and updating real-time shipment statuses to customers

- Efficiently organize multiple deliveries

- Improve the business through innovative sales strategies

- Mediate and resolve freight inconsistencies and challenges

Marketing and Communication

Your business must be visible if you are to make money in this industry. For that to happen, you will have to invest in a proper marketing campaign. There are many marketing tools and resources you can use to make this happen. Here are some of your duties:

- Constant communication with shippers to update them on the delivery progress

- Networking and maintaining positive relationships with relevant stakeholders

- Discussing and negotiating price agreements with different carriers

- Reach out to current and former shippers and carriers for new business

- Lead generation

- Building and reviewing the sales pipeline

Later in this book, we will discuss in-depth how to market your brokerage firm, including successful strategies that have been used by brokers over the years.

Maintaining paperwork

It is your legal obligation as a freight broker to process and maintain paperwork for all the transactions. For compliance purposes, you are expected to maintain paperwork for transactions for at least three years, during which shippers and carriers can go through and verify the information for whichever purpose.

Besides the legal requirements, you must also ascertain that all the freight paperwork involving transactions under your brokerage firm are duly filed and approved before you engage carriers for transportation services.

How Will I Make Money?

The logistics industry is one of the wealthiest, with billions of dollars in cargo value being transported daily. It is also an industry with many players, from shippers, carriers, brokers and other agents, all of who share in the pie. Before you start your brokerage firm, you definitely want to know how you will get paid for your effort.

As an intermediary, most of your work is no different from a salesman. However, the difference is that freight brokers are generally paid based on the gross load margin instead of the gross revenues. This is because, in this industry, gross revenues are not considered as the underlying metrics. Profits in freight brokerage are realized as a function of each buy or sell transaction that you make. To understand this, we must consider the relationship between gross margins and gross revenue.

Gross revenue in this industry is the earnings you make from charges levied to shippers (your customers). The difference between your charges to shippers and what you pay carriers is the gross margin. We can represent this in a simple equation as follows:

Gross margin = Price charged to shipper – Price paid to carriers

The difference you get from this equation represents the real value of profitability for each transaction. Note that the distinction between these two charges is important in freight brokerage just as much as it is in determining your brokerage commission.

The last thing you want to do is address your earnings as a function of gross revenues. This can be so deceptive and will never give you the true picture. The freight brokerage industry is different from other industries because in those industries, the cost of manufacturing or services rendered is usually stable, albeit relatively. On the other hand, the cost of hiring carriers is determined by a lot of factors, most of which change all the time. Let's use an example to explain this further:

$10,000 charged to shipper – $9,000 paid to the carrier = $1000 gross margin or net revenue

$4,000 charged to shipper − $3,000 paid to the carrier = $1000 gross margin or net revenue

If you look at the figures above, the gross revenue is higher in the $10,000 load, but in the real sense, each of the loads brings in the same gross margin.

Another term that is used to describe gross margins is net revenue. In accounting and finance terms, net is usually the term used to determine the profits you retain after making all allowable deductions, in this case, what you collect from shippers once you pay carriers to move the cargo to their destination.

The other difference between the freight brokerage industry and other industries, especially those where tangible goods are produced, is that the freight industry's transportation cost is often volatile. Because of this, the role of a freight broker is more or less similar to a financial broker. You buy and sell assets based on the prevailing market conditions and earn a commission for the services rendered.

This is the same model that is employed by most online retail platforms like eBay. As much as billions of dollars are transacted on their platforms, they earn a commission on each transaction value. Therefore, their commissions are their net revenues after accounting for payroll costs, administrative, marketing, technology and any other functions.

Whether you sell $400,000 or $40,000 to shippers in freight brokerage, this is immaterial to determining your commissions earned. Besides, commissions and compensation vary from one broker to the next. Since every broker can set their rates according to their business model and other considerations, there is no universal commission plan. Depending on how your brokerage business works, some brokers earn a base salary and commissions, while others are only paid on commission as a gross margin of loads.

Chapter 2
Is It Worth It?

Going into any business, one of the common doubts people usually have is whether they are making the right choice. Granted, you are investing a lot of money, probably most of your savings into the business, so it is only fair that you should know your investment will be safe. In light of the recent coronavirus pandemic, many people have held back on investments, and for a good reason. If you heed financial advisors and analysts' advice, you must be prudent in your investments as we advance.

What does this mean for the freight brokerage market? Regardless of their opinions, most analysts and experts on freight and logistics believe that as much as 2020 was a year full of uncertainties, the freight industry was shaken up like every other industry, but for its resilience, it has grown and will keep growing over the next couple of years.

There are many reasons for the sustained growth in this industry. One of these is the continued growth of online retail. With more businesses operating online, many people operate the back end side of their businesses from warehouses. They market and engage customers online, but goods are delivered from their warehouses to the customer. If you expand on this to the context of interstate and international trade, you can begin to understand why the freight industry keeps growing and the prospect for freight brokers.

Coming into the year 2020, North America was the biggest freight brokerage market, and this trend is widely expected to persist over the coming years. Other brokerage markets of interest include Canada and Mexico.

As the industry's middle man, your role is to link trucking companies and shippers with customers. As the industry grows, systemic challenges further shift attention to freight brokers' role. One of these is the shortage of truck drivers in the market. In light of the pandemic, many truck drivers have been unable to carry out their duties. The shortage of drivers meant that brokers had to increase the cost of getting goods to shippers as demand increased for the few truck drivers available.

On their end, it is only natural for shippers to find more affordable brokers whose pricing is within an acceptable range. An interesting feature of the freight brokerage market is that it usually feels changes in other related industries. For example, as the e-commerce world grows, so does the need for long-distance freight delivery.

When companies like Amazon launch their brokerage service, you know the market is ripe for exponential growth. The value proposition for Amazon freight brokerage, for example, is that shippers can easily get quotes and match with a carrier right away. Their entry into the digital brokerage service matches customers' demand for shipping with the available trucking capacity. With other digital competitors, like Transfix, Convoy and Uber Freight, already in the industry, this is proof that there is room for anyone who can offer value to the customers.

Amazon uses their wealth in artificial intelligence to match available freight needs and trucker capacity, such that in the long run, customers enjoy cost savings and efficiency. It is not just about the large freight shipments. Amazon has also expanded its capacity to deliver smaller packages, offering last-mile delivery to its customers.

Now, suppose you consider the fact that Amazon has quite the experience in delivering shipments all over the world. In that case, their entry into the brokerage market gives them an edge over not so innovative brokers. Their operation's sheer size puts them at an advantage because they can offer highly competitive prices and, more importantly, a streamlined freight delivery service.

So, is it still worth it, investing in freight brokerage, to compete with giants like Amazon? Yes, it is. You might not be able to compete with them muscle-for-muscle, but you can learn from their approach, innovate and offer incredible value to your customers. Indeed, large brokers can offer excellent prices, but their size comes with unique challenges that could have been avoided by using a relatively smaller broker. For example, how many times have you heard people complaining about losing one or a few of their packages that should have arrived from Amazon? Large companies can offer so much, but simple things like these make some customers shy away from them and prefer smaller brokers who can give them the best services and listen to their concerns.

Growth Projections

The freight market is a highly fragmented industry, and for this reason, players in the market must come up with different growth approaches. Over the years, participants in the market have had to leverage drivers like demand for transport and logistics services to spur growth opportunities in the market. With more opportunities for growth and the impact of the global pandemic, everyone involved in the freight industry, including carriers, shippers and brokers, has to focus on a growth prospect in a fast-growth market while at the same time cementing their position in the slow-growth segments.

Increased activity in the manufacturing sector raised more risks and complexities in the supply chain. Due to this, many industries have since realized the benefit of working with freight brokers to streamline goods' transportation. In this capacity, brokers essentially design, manage and optimize the distribution network to ensure that goods are delivered on time from the source to the destination and in good condition. For the end-users, this translates to reduced operational costs.

As the demand for transport and logistics services increases from most of the end-user industries like e-commerce, manufacturing, pharmaceutical, auto and FMCG, it is expected that the demand for freight brokerage will increase in equal measure, with a compounded annual growth rate of at least 4% in the period up to 2024.

Another possible reason for growing demand is the increase in low-cost manufacturing products from countries like Mexico, Brazil, China and South Africa. It is widely expected that this will further increase demand for freight brokerage in North America, given that the products from these countries have favorable markets in the US.

In particular, growth in the e-commerce sector is one factor that has led to an increase in the less than load (LTL) freight market. LTL refers to the transportation of small cargo that does not warrant a full truckload. Shippers generally consolidate a lot of LTL cargo in one truck and have them transported to different destinations. In this case, a freight broker's role is to organize and plan the delivery route for the carrier, in the process fully maximizing the capacity of that truck. Through LTL freight, you minimize shipping costs and reduce carbon emissions, which many players in the industry currently value.

Technological Disruption

Technology is bound to play an essential role in the growth of the freight brokerage industry. From what we have seen in the past, everyone in the industry is looking at integrating some aspect of disruptive technology into their business. In particular, shippers are in a good position to optimize their shipping schedules and reduce costs in the process. On the other hand, carriers make the most use of their haulage assets.

Tech companies are also making their mark in the industry. Take Uber Technologies, for example. Since the launch of Uber Freight in 2017, more than 400,000 drivers across 36,000 carriers have been contracted on the app, serving thousands of shippers' needs. Other companies that have joined the fray include Convoy, Transfix and Loadsmart. Each of these companies has invested in algorithms that help shippers find carriers to transport their loads efficiently.

Of course, this is one of those tech disruptions that will challenge traditional brokerage firms. What you need to do is to embrace technology and stay relevant in the market. No one likes delays when it comes to transport and logistics, so the best move for you would be to align yourself with such technological advancements.

Apart from the tech giants entering the market, even traditional brokers in the industry have embraced technology in one way or the other. To remain competitive and relevant in the market, carriers have also picked up on the trend and adapted them into their operations. This tells you that, apart from learning about the freight brokerage's ins and outs, you also need to learn about the tech aspect so that you have a clear path laid out by the time you go in.

Competitive Advantage

The transportation management industry is currently enjoying a competitive advantage in light of increased tech disruption. This can be seen in freight brokerage markets and third-party logistics sectors. While tech can be seen as a disruptor, it has also leveled the playing field for brokers. For small and medium-sized brokers, the technological disruption is a welcome advancement because it allows them to stay competitive in the market, notwithstanding large brokerage firms' efforts.

Technology plays a vital role in brokerage. First, it helps with visibility and allows brokers to use freight matching to cover more loads efficiently. This is something that small brokers have struggled with over the years compared to more prominent brokers. The automation process improves your effectiveness such that you can now handle more business than you would with a manual system.

Another area where technology has assisted small brokers is shipment visibility. This means that your customers are now in an excellent position to know more about their shipment remotely. This means you no longer have to keep calling them with updates. Real-time shipment tracking has made work easier for brokers and given shippers peace of mind. On the part of the carriers, they are fully aware of the role technology plays throughout the haulage period, so they strive to make deliveries on schedule. Such changes free up more time for you to spend on managing your business, marketing, focusing on growth, networking and any other aspect of your business, thereby leveling the playing field and allowing you to grow just as fast as larger brokers.

Finally, one of the areas where tech brings a competitive advantage is automated invoicing. Forget about the days of manual invoicing where a lot of time and energy would be lost. Automated invoicing increases efficiency and has also reduced the lag between cargo delivery and payment, which traditionally made business difficult for many small brokers. As long as you were not getting your invoices paid on time, you would end up with piling and expensive debt, and in the long run, shutting down was the best option since small brokers did not have the financial muscle that larger brokers had in the industry.

Essentially, by leveling the playing field for small and large brokers alike, the competitive advantage is a win-win situation for everyone. Back in the day, shippers had a difficult time trusting small brokers. There was the concern that a broker can wake up one day and close their operation for lack of funds. Today, however, automated invoicing means that brokers get paid on time and can handle most shippers' business regardless of their size. Besides, through LTL freight, many shippers embrace the concept of consolidation, significantly reducing the cost of delivery to their destinations. It is safe to say that the technological disruption has fostered trust between shippers, freight brokers and carriers.

Going forward, you must have a clear vision of what to do and how to go about starting your brokerage firm. You need to know how to set competitive prices and, more importantly, how to reach out to customers. In the coming chapters, we will discuss in-depth how to make your mark in this industry. From segmenting the market and finding your niche, writing a business plan and finding shippers and carriers, we will cover everything you need to know. If you have never written a business plan before, we will also work on a template you can use to create your first.

So, is it really worth it, investing your time and money into freight brokerage? Yes, it is. Before you begin, however, you must take time and learn the basics of this industry. Like any other business, you cannot go in blindly and hope to succeed.

This is a considerable investment on your part, and it is only fair that you give it the attention it deserves.

Chapter 3
The Importance of Knowing Your Target Market

In the earlier chapters, we mentioned the importance of connections and networks in the freight brokerage business. Adding to that, it is worth mentioning that this is an industry where your reputation is equally important. Reliability is one of the essential traits that will get you the kind of attention you need to grow your venture. Carriers need assurances that you will always pay their dues on time. Shippers, on the other hand, are more concerned about the safety of their cargo.

It might feel like this kind of reputation is only achievable after being in the industry for years, but that is not necessarily true. You can actually kickstart your career within the first year by understanding your market and shifting your focus to specific segments. With some research, you can identify sectors that are underserved by large firms in the market. You will also learn some of the challenges that the established firms have in meeting such groups' needs and capitalize on them. This is the principle of niche marketing.

Niche (Micro) Marketing

It is easier to grow your freight brokerage business by identifying a niche and focusing on meeting your customers' needs. Naturally, when you start this operation, it might seem like you are shifting your attention from the wider market, but that is not the case. Focusing on a select group makes it easier to understand and address their concerns better. It is also one of the most reliable ways of keeping a steady flow of business.

Benefits of Niche Marketing

The fact that you serve a given market segment daily gives you a better perspective of the players in that sector and their needs. With this understanding, you are better placed to address unique needs that large companies can't due to the diseconomies of scale. This experience and expertise go a long way in building customer trust, confidence and growing a reputation for your business and your brand. If you diligently keep at it, you will end up with a network of reliable carriers, shippers, and other strategic partners, like bankers, who help you grow your brokerage business.

Generally, niche marketing allows you to avoid wastage through special marketing efforts. Instead of scattering your marketing effort everywhere, you focus on an approach that will yield results. Broad marketing involves a lot of wastage because, most of the time, the majority of the recipients barely listen to you. Through niche marketing, you can use tools like emotional appeals to reach a specific audience.

- **High return on investment (ROI)**

By shifting your marketing efforts to a specific target group, you address their needs better, making them more likely to do business with you than conventional advertisers. In the beginning, it might seem counterproductive to have a smaller target audience, but with time, you realize that your conversion rate is better than a broad marketing approach. This is how to get and maintain a high ROI.

Apart from the customer approach, niche marketing is also easier on your budget. Compared to mass marketing, you spend less on niche marketing, even if you use the same marketing outlets. For example, TV ads cost more for a wider audience, when in the real sense, most of them will not pay attention to you.

- **Brand visibility**

Niche marketing helps you to improve your presence in the industry by enhancing your visibility. Generally, businesses that serve a niche market tend to offer unique services, making them stand out. In this way, you have an opportunity to present yourself before the right customers, which makes more business sense than presenting yourself in front of the mass market. The more people who are aware of your services, the higher the likelihood they will recommend you to their friends, families and associates, especially if their needs align with your offering.

- **Customer loyalty**

If there is one reason why you should consider niche marketing, it is customer loyalty. By design, niche marketing helps you to put the needs of your customers first. You listen to them and take care of their needs better than the more prominent companies can. Through niche marketing, you can address customer concerns at a personal level. Remember, we talked about this being an industry that's big on networking and connections. Customer loyalty plays a huge role in this.

Besides, by offering unique services to your customers, you stand out from the competition.

● Growth through word of mouth

Niche marketing is big on word of mouth advertising. You will realize that people in a given niche are often in contact with one another. It is more or less similar to creating a close-knit community around your brokerage service. This gives you more opportunities to talk about your business and introduce new services to your clientele. For example, if the shippers or carriers express some concern to which you have a unique solution, they will soon become your best brand ambassadors. By serving them better and offering unique solutions, you can earn recommendations from their circles.

● Less competition

You will encounter less competition in niche mass marketing. From the onset, you start your brokerage firm on a growth trajectory. Mass marketing does work, but it is more effective for larger companies and brands that have been in the market longer. Bearing this in mind, you can consider mass marketing once you grow your brand.

● Improved experiences

In principle, niche marketing demands a concentrated approach in a given sector. This means that you will hone your expertise in a short time and become an expert in the field. Take note that most customers are enticed by your knowledge and experience in the field over the brand name. When you become an expert in a field, you will earn more than the customers' trust, and you also get brand recognition in the process.

Doing everything that everyone else is doing can only make you an average freight broker, at best. That's the risk of blending in with the crowd. However, if you are bold enough to focus on solving typical shipper and carrier problems better and faster than everyone else, you will stand out.

Possible Challenges in Niche Marketing

You should not take niche marketing as a blanket strategy for growing your business even with these benefits. As successful as niche marketing is for your business, there are some risks that you must be aware of. You need customers to grow, and by narrowing down your attention to a niche, you have a better chance of growing your brand faster. However, you are basically attending to a smaller market through niche marketing, which translates to slower or stunted growth. Given your demographic limits, it might take you longer to scale the heights you envisioned in your business plan.

- **Market vulnerability**

Venturing into niche marketing means taking more risks than the average freight broker. You peg all your hopes on succeeding with this niche approach. The challenge here is that you are putting all your eggs in one basket. While niche marketing can be a springboard to success, you are more vulnerable to drastic changes in the market, especially those that do not favor your target audience.

Another challenge with this vulnerability is that as much as it carries the prospect of a higher ROI, that return is not guaranteed. Because of the small market size, you might struggle to make large profit margins. It will be even harder to expand your market share. Besides, the concept of niche marketing means fewer customers, which might be a risky prospect for a new business.

- **Innovation risk**

If you decide to go with niche marketing, you must find a way to innovate. In niche marketing, you go against the norm, especially when everyone else is using mass marketing. You will end up with a uniquely segmented market, and for lack of competition, it becomes difficult to know whether or not you need to improve your services. After all, there are not many competitors pushing your brand to do better.

- **The success conundrum**

The whole point of niche marketing is to succeed in your venture. However, success comes at a price. If your marketing approach proves successful, you can expect increased interest and competition from other brokers, and from there, it won't be long before your niche is saturated.

In retrospect, there are always advantages and disadvantages to every business model. However, you need customers to grow your business. You cannot do anything because of the disadvantages of niche marketing. Learning about them helps you to preempt their occurrence and act accordingly. For a beginner freight broker, the best way to make a name for yourself in such a highly competitive industry is niche marketing. Monitor the market, grow your influence and as your reputation grows, you can scale up your marketing approach accordingly.

How to Choose a Niche

With the knowledge you have on niche marketing, the next step is choosing your brokerage firm's right niche. There are many ways to go about this. Some people learn to identify niches while going through freight broker training. Others know their target market much earlier. If you do not fall into either of these categories, do not despair. The gist of niche selection has nothing to do with the industry but is a personal assessment.

- **Personal assessment**

Evaluate your level of preparedness before you begin. This is where your personality comes in. Think in terms of your talent, interest, skills, and personality. This is not just to help you select the niche, but it will also help you stay motivated when things are not going according to plan, which in business can happen to anyone.

Starting a business is one of the most difficult things you can do. Many people have all the necessary resources and opportunities but never have the guts to go ahead. You are in a good place because you have taken the first step, starting the business. So, how do you apply your personal assessment to discover your niche? List down your passions, knowledge, skills and expertise. There are many niches out there, and choosing one you are not knowledgeable about or passionate about is the first step towards failure. We need to avoid that.

Choose a niche you understand, not just because it is interesting. In business, things get tough from time to time and passion subsides. Ask yourself whether you see yourself working in that niche over the next five or seven years.

How does your skill level and past experience come into play? Think of what you learned before and how you can use it to gain an advantage in the niche. In some cases, you might need additional training to fit into the niche that you desire.

- **Market research**

Your work doesn't end when you realize that your personal traits align with the desired niche. It doesn't end when you select the niche, either. You have to research and determine whether there is a market for that particular niche. In freight brokerage, there are many niches you can consider. For example, you can segment the market in terms of special cargo, regional niches, types of trucks you use, or the type of material or products that are shipped through your brokerage firm.

Next, you want to understand the unique value proposition your firm is offering customers. What makes you different from other brokers? Why should shippers work with you instead of other brokers? What do you offer that others do not? This is where you understand your strengths and gain an in-depth understanding of the competitors' weaknesses. It also helps you to know where your business will be more effective.

Passion for your business and the selected niche will only get you so far. Be careful not to choose a niche with a tiny customer base. This is important because, ultimately, your business will only be and remain viable to customers when you address their needs. Let's say, for example, that you are a huge fan of motorbikes. You can research and find out how they are handled from one point to the next, and narrow down your business concept. Find out whether demand and supply in the market is sustainable over time.

Your advantage, in this case, comes from knowledge and experience. Since you know so much about motorbikes and you are an enthusiast, you can easily offer unique services to shippers and carriers than someone else who lacks your kind of knowledge might not be able to offer.

- **Geographical niches**

One method that has worked for many freight brokers in the past is to focus on regional niches. It is easier to find customers within your region. You can consider the state or even your city. Study the market and understand the core businesses in your region. If you are a manufacturing hub, you can specialize in handling those products. It gets even better if you enjoy some of the manufactured or assembled things in your region.

At the same time, try not to spread yourself thin. While enthusiasm is a good thing, only take up businesses that you can handle, or you will damage your reputation. Do not commit to loads that you cannot handle to fulfill the customers' satisfaction.

- **Types of trucks and cargo**

Another method of niche selection is to consider the type of trucks used. There is quite a variety you can work with, including tankers, flatbeds, dry vans and so on. Start with the kind of truck you can handle comfortably and make a name for yourself in the process. This way it is easier to find carriers and shippers with whom to partner.

In the same way you considered different types of trucks, consider the types of cargo. Every type of cargo requires a unique handling procedure. For example, the procedure for handling motorbike cargo is not the same as dairy, meat, or eggs. This gives you a lot of room for consideration. Delicate and perishable goods like dairy, meat and eggs need special handling.

If you start with these, you will have to look for special trucks that can transport the cargo without a hitch. You also have to look for carriers who are comfortable transporting that kind of cargo. In many cases, shippers tend to give special instructions for handling such delicate products, so you can use that as a stepping stone to making your mark in that niche.

When serving a particular niche, you become an expert over time. Before you know it, you become the go-to guy in your space for certain types of cargo. Once you've established a reputation for solid dependability, your reach becomes much more significant.

There's one danger in niche marketing, though—you can become so focused that your total revenue could end up coming from a few sources. Learn from the niche haulers of the trucking industry. Less than 25%–30% of their revenues come from a single source; they keep it diversified even within the niche. With the vagaries of the economy, putting your eggs in one basket can spell disaster when something terrible happens, a reality that even large freight broker companies are not immune to.

The following are some essential questions whose answers will lead you in the right direction during niche selection:

1. What products or companies are you interested in? Do you have a close connection to those brands?

2. What do you know about the logistics operation of the brands that interest you? Are their most pressing needs currently being met? If not, what can you do to fulfill their needs better than any other broker?

3. What are the best sources of information on the companies, brands, or products you want to serve? What can you do to become an expert in the field?

4. Who benefits most from your brokerage service?

5. Can you profile your ideal customer? What are their needs, strengths and weaknesses? How do you benefit their operation by being their niche broker?

From your answers to these questions, you can draft a plan to reach out to the customers you have profiled. Find out the key decision-makers for the companies and brands, and get in touch with them.

Ahead of your meeting, prepare a brief introduction for your brokerage firm, highlighting the value you bring to their operation and how having you as their go-to broker will benefit their overall business strategy. The introduction aims to show them how you will prop their success, helping them streamline their operation. If you can do that, you will have them on board.

Is it possible to have more than one niche?

The market is so wide, and there are many niches that you can tap into. So, the answer to the question above is yes! You can immerse yourself in more than one niche. It does not matter that you are new to the brokerage industry. Take note, however, that the concept of niche marketing is about perfection. Invest your time in one niche, perfect it, and use the lessons and skills learned to grow into another niche.

Working towards more than one niche is a growth-minded approach that means you will continuously be looking for opportunities to diversify your brokerage business. With time, your business will grow, and in the process, it will be easier for you to find niches that are a natural fit to your expertise.

Growing niches can only mean one thing; that you are doing great. Customers who grow with you in your journey will most likely send you referrals, helping your business to grow exponentially, too.

The thing about niche marketing in the freight brokerage industry is that there are times when you will need to think outside the box. One example of this is learning how to use keywords to your advantage. Keywords are not only for online businesses. When marketing your freight brokerage business, you use all the tools available at your disposal. An essential tool in your arsenal is keyword research.

Keyword research helps you to determine how often people search for specific phrases online. You can also identify seasonal trends of those and related searches and use that information to identify the right niche in the process. You will look at impressions, clicks, and the value attached to them. This sounds like search engine optimization, but it is useful. If a few people are searching for particular keywords, they are probably low-value keywords. The lesson here is that there is not much in that niche to warrant your attention. It could be too niche, and you would price yourself out of the market.

As we advance, always know that your niche's ideal definition should correspond with you and your business' needs. You can use standard industry benchmarks for general insight and leave it at that because your competitors are probably not doing the same thing.

In terms of marketing your freight brokerage firm, there isn't much to choose between niche marketing and mass marketing. It all comes down to what is right at that moment. They are both effective, depending on how you use them. What's mandatory on your part is proper planning, research, and with the right tools, you can use niche marketing to grow your brokerage firm and become the brand everyone wants to work with.

Chapter 4
Let's Talk About Money

The freight brokerage industry is the backbone of many businesses in the country. Before going into this business, you should be aware of the costs involved to plan your finances accordingly. One of the first things you should think about is the location of your business. Today, many people work from home, in light of the recent pandemic. If you find this appropriate, it will save you on office setup costs. That being said, you might want to lease an office, in which case there will be other costs to look at. If you are hiring a team of employees, you will also have to plan for salaries and other related expenses.

Start-up Costs

So, the biggest question on your mind is how much you should set aside to start your freight brokerage business. The total sum varies from one individual to the next, depending on your preferences. To make your work easier, let's look at the components of your expenditure list and, at the end of this chapter, we will determine the total cost of setting up.

Business Registration

You must first register the business with the Secretary of State, from where you will receive a tax number and registration from the department of revenue in your state. Assuming you will also operate as a carrier, you must get a permit from the DMV. The total registration costs vary from one state to the next and cost up to $300. Other costs, including that of registering a tax number, are set differently by each state.

Brokerage License

Upon application, the Federal Motor Carrier Safety Administration (FMCSA) grants you the license to operate as a freight broker. This is to certify your qualifications and authorizes you to operate as a freight broker or carrier.

You can apply for this license in two categories: a property broker or household goods broker. While you can apply for whichever suits your needs, it makes sense to apply for both and a carrier license if you have your own trucks. The license fee is $300 for each of the authorities.

On top of that, you also need to set aside $60–$80 for the annual Unified Carrier Registration (UCR), which applies to freight carriers and brokers.

Annual Surety Bond

To protect all the stakeholders' interests in the industry, the FMCSA set a surety bond of $75,000, which is an agreement between the freight broker, surety company, and authorities. The surety bond is safeguarded against any form of misconduct that any of the parties might suffer if the freight broker breaches set industry rules and regulations. Note, however, that both your business and yourself are not protected under this surety. It is basically to protect your customers and the licensing authority.

$75,000 sounds steep for someone who is just setting up a business, right? Well, you only have to pay a fraction of it. The amount you pay will depend on your credit rating, industry experience, and financial history on other credit facilities you might have. People with a good credit score can pay up to 4% ($3000), and as low as 1% ($750) annually. With bad credit, you can pay up to 12% ($9000) annually. If you start at 12%, you can reduce your annual premiums by working on improving your credit.

Cargo and Liability Insurance (Optional)

It is good practice to get insurance when going into a business. According to the FMCSA, however, getting cargo, liability, or property insurance is not mandatory. So, what should you do? Think in terms of insurance value. There's that peace of mind, knowing that you are protected in the event of freight damage or an irresponsible carrier. While this insurance cover is optional, having it gives your shippers confidence that yours is a legitimate business—this can earn you more business.

On average, insurance policies for cargo will cost around $1500 a year. You might also spend a similar amount on property and liability policies. Note, however, that if you hire employees, it is mandatory to have workers' compensation insurance.

While a surety bond protects the authorities and your customers, you are protected by the business insurance cover you take. Other than workers' compensation, other forms of business insurance you can take include property insurance and general liability coverage. If you are working from home, talk to your insurer about a relevant home-based insurance cover.

Office and Office Equipment

The cost of setting up an office depends on the kind of equipment you need. On average, you can set up a small office for around $1000. Next, you will look at monthly recurring expenditures, including assorted equipment, stationery, and utility bills. For this, you can expect to spend around $500.

Office expenses largely depend on the type of setup you are working with. Thinking of office space, working from home will significantly reduce your expenditure. Most brokers today use their personal phones to keep in touch with business partners. With a laptop and a small desk at home, you might cut out a massive chunk from your office and equipment budget.

Speaking of your laptop or computer, you don't need something fancy. A device with 8GB of RAM and a core i5 processor should be more than sufficient. Building on that, you need proper storage. Today, there are lots of cloud storage options you can use, both premium and freemium services. This will help you with regular backups, so your data is always safe.

Licensed Brokerage Software

While they are not mandatory, look into brokerage software. We live in a world where you cannot ignore the disruptive impact and importance of technology in your industry. Software solutions exist to make your work easier. The complete package should include a transportation management system (TMS) and a customer relationship manager (CRM). You will also need a load board to connect you with available and qualified carriers for cargo. So far, most players in the industry swear by DAT and TruckStop. You can sign up for a load board for around $50.

These software solutions offer greater efficiency in managing your business. You can start with simple software solutions and scale up as your business grows. On average, you should spend between $1000 and $3000 on software annually.

Training

While freight brokerage training is optional, it will be useful if you have never worked in the industry in any capacity before, either as a motor carrier or a broker. Some of the skills you will learn include compliance with legal guidelines in your jurisdiction and how to manage the brokerage firm. The training cost varies from one institution to the other, the course content and material, and range from $200 to $1500, or higher.

Marketing

Marketing is key to the growth of your freight brokerage business. Considering the importance of establishing strong networks, you must find a way to promote your business. Referrals and word of mouth will work, and for the most part, they are effective. However, these are highly effective if you have an established network of customers and other transportation industry professionals.

For a new business, you will have to pay for marketing services. Towards this end, plan for a website, attend networking events and try to join load boards. You can also use your social media outlets. You can get a simple website from $300 onwards. While in the design stage, ensure your developer builds a website that loads fast and offers users all the information they need at a glance.

Accounting Tools

You will need to account for the way money moves in and out of your business. This is where accounting tools are useful. One option is to hire an accountant to help you either on a full-time basis or on a contract basis. However, if you do not have that much money to spare, many accounting tools are simple, easy to use and affordable. One of these is QuickBooks.

QuickBooks is so easy to use, you don't need accounting experience to make the most use of it. You can also find tutorial videos online and on YouTube that will give you the best introduction to the accounting suite. Accounting tools are essential in your business because they help you to prepare clean financial records. On average, you might spend around $50 a month on this, depending on the suite you use.

From our discussion above, we can now summarize the estimated costs of setting up your operation as follows:

- Rent: $0–$1,000

- Equipment: $6,000–$22,000

- Licenses/tax deposits: $200–$400

- Advertising/marketing: $500–$1,500

- Utilities/phone: $100–$300

- Professional services: $200–$750

- Payroll: $0–$5,000

- Supplies: $300–$500

- Insurance (first quarter): $700–$1,400

- Suggested operating capital: $5,000–$250,000 (cash or line of credit)

Remember that these costs are just estimates, meant to guide you. The actual figures will depend on different features, especially your location and personal preferences for your operation.

The Profit

Going into any business, one of the most important things to consider is profit. It is not just about how much you will make from the business but, more importantly, about sustainability. Note that unless you explicitly register your business as such, you are neither a shipper nor a carrier but a middleman who ensures the aforementioned parties have their needs met. Since your work ensures carriers earn more money by keeping their trucks full and shippers get access to reliable carriers, the next step is to look into the profit margins. Let's make one thing clear: Unless you are employed under someone, you do not earn a salary in this industry. Brokers earn commissions.

According to the U.S Bureau of Labor Statistics projections, the future is bright for freight brokers. The industry has been on an upward growth trajectory. This means there is more room for you to make money.

How much do I take home?

One of the top questions on your mind is probably how much you will earn in this business. Given that freight brokers earn commissions, it is virtually impractical to calculate an accurate annual income. That notwithstanding, PayScale, Indeed and Glassdoor estimate that freight brokers bring in anywhere between $30,000 and $92000 a year. Many factors determine how much you earn in this industry, so it is possible to earn much more or even less. For example, brokers in the bigger cities, like Portland and Kansas City, earn more than their counterparts in the smaller cities. This is due to things like the volume and frequency of business you can conduct in a given time.

That being said, the national average annual earnings for freight brokers is around $62,105. On commission, you can rake in an extra $28,000 every year.

This is an industry where your earnings are directly proportional to your input and effort into the business. Many freight brokers earn six-figure salaries, yet they work from home. This caliber of brokers has a good reputation and have been in the business longer. You can join that league by taking your work seriously. You can grow your business and have agents working for you for commissions of up to 15%.

The figures above notwithstanding, your average income comes down to factors like your experience level, your customers' profitability, your gross revenue, business structure and reputation in the market. To understand this better, let's look at your position in terms of the three types of brokers in the industry below. The assumption here is that each of the brokers conducts the same amount of business. For the purpose of this discussion, we will assume an annual revenue of $2,000,000, and with a 17.5% margin, an annual gross profit of $350,000.

1. **The W-2 Broker**

You will realize that there are more W-2 brokers in the market than all the other categories, with most large freight brokerage companies operating in this category. Practically, this is a company that hires personnel in different sales and operations capacities. They also own the customer accounts and run all the business operations but offer the brokers office space.

As a W-2 broker, you might earn a basic salary and a commission based on your company's profits. On average, W-2 brokers earn around $40,000, with an extra 13% in commission of the gross profits.

From our sales and gross profit projections earlier, at 13%, your annual income translates to:

$40,000 + $45,500 = $85,500

Why should you consider getting into the business as a W-2 broker? Well, since you will be an employee, you are on a payroll and like every other employee, you earn a basic salary. The base salary gives you a guarantee, especially if you are new to the industry and are uncertain about your productivity. The commissions are a bonus based on your effort and input into the business. Another benefit is that most companies will pay for your training courses.

That being said, your employer retains most of the profit, and you might also have to sign a non-compete clause in your contract to protect your employer's interests and to prevent you from moving to a competitor with their customers.

2. The Licensed Broker

A licensed broker is a business owner, meaning that you will assume all the risks associated with the business. With all the necessary assets, you can scale the business accordingly over the years. Operating as a licensed owner means there is as great a chance of success as there is of failure. There are no independent contractors or employees.

In this case, you must be licensed by the Department of Transportation. As discussed earlier, you will also obtain a surety bond and apply for all other services necessary to run the business, including insurance. We discussed most of the costs that you will incur earlier in this chapter. The challenge comes in realizing how much you have to invest in the business without earning anything yet.

For licensed brokers, costs typically pile up so fast, so you might have to look into additional means of financing the operation. Most successful licensed brokers have loyal customers. It is your responsibility to run all the business functions, or hire staff to assist, where necessary. This model's beauty is that you enjoy 100% of what remains after accounting for expenses and other relevant deductions. You also shoulder 100% of the burden if you are making losses.

Many licensed brokers fold up in less than three years because they don't have sufficient recurring revenue to keep the business running or insufficient start-up cash. Here's what your financial year might look like:

Total operating expenses

DoT Authorities	$300
Bond	$10,000
Insurance	$3,000
Software	$7,500
Load boards	$3,600
Factoring	$70,000
Wages	$40,000
Total	**$134,400**

Profit & Loss Assessment

Revenue	$2,000,000
Carriers	($1,650,000)
Gross profit	**$350000**
Expenses	($134,400)
Net Earnings	**$215,600**

In this example, you take home $215,600 annually.

3. **The 1099 Agent**

In this category, you work as an independent contractor, but for a licensed broker. This category has grown relatively popular in recent years. The licensed broker assumes all the costs discussed above, but the broker business is handled either by an agent, or a group of agents.

Most of your work involves finding freight and moving it through carriers, so you can pretty much work from home. The licensed agent handles all the back-office tasks like marketing, claims handling, billing, tech support, collections, etc. Your role as an agent is restricted to sales and operations, which you can also sub-contract if you need to.

While this model offers more flexibility than the other two, it is not your best bet as a beginner. You must bring in your customers and organize their schedules, including the dispatch trucks. Earnings in this category are commission-based, with some of the top agents earning up to 70%, with the licensed broker retaining the rest to cover business expenses. On average, 1099 agents can take home more than $200,000 a year.

Having looked at all the categories, which one works for you? More importantly, you can now understand the difference in earning structures for freight brokers. As exciting as these figures are, you must also note that they were hypothetical. It might take you a while to earn $2 million, probably not in your first year of operation. Since you do not have to deal with office logistics, many brokers today operate as 1099 agents, using the resources saved to focus on growing their customer database.

The Pricing

Having discussed the costs and possible profit margins, you need to take a closer look at the money. One of the most important relationships that will help you to succeed is with your banker. You need a good relationship with your banker to succeed in the freight brokerage business. You will need a line of credit to pay carriers before you receive anything from the shippers from time to time. With a good relationship, you can count on your banker for a quick $300,000 in such times. Note that without securing carriers' payment on time, they will avoid your freight. Without carriers, you have no business. Therefore, as much as you will be looking at insurance, licenses and other costs, you should prioritize finding a good banker who understands your business's nature and can assist on short notice.

How do you handle this? First, a bank you have never done business with will be apprehensive. Even your usual bank will be apprehensive if you do not have a business plan. Another factor that will make things easier for you is your credit record. This is important because the freight brokers typically do not have any assets the bank can repossess if you default on payments. Your business plan should include a profile package that shows the bank you are creditworthy and, by opening a line of credit for you, they will also get good business in return.

That being said, how do you determine freight charges? These are generally based on the load weight and the distance the carriers will move it. Other factors that determine freight charges include the type of truck requested for that particular cargo and the number of stops the driver must make to pick up and deliver the load.

Shipments are generally moved on a one pickup one delivery basis without incurring additional charges. If the carrier must make extra stops, you can discuss and negotiate the terms and charges with them. It is wise to study the market and know the prevailing shipping rates and specifications for the kind of cargo you will haul. Contact a few carriers and compare their rates and tariffs for this.

Since you are paid on commission, you can either bill the shipper the carrier's cost plus your commission or have the carrier bill the shipper and then pay your commission. Since the latter is cumbersome, most freight brokers bill customers after the carrier bills them. Note that while commissions are negotiable, they are not the net earnings. Commissions earned are part of your gross earnings. From there, you must account for overheads like rent, debts, utility bills, sales commissions, payroll processing, taxes and so on.

Chapter 5
Writing a Business Plan

A business plan is an important step towards the success of your brokerage firm. This is a plan that gives an in-depth description of your business. Investors and financiers generally look at your business plan to determine whether your business is sound enough to warrant their support. We mentioned earlier in the book that you need to have a good relationship with your banker in this industry. From time to time, you will need a line of credit to keep things running. Without a business plan, your bank cannot ascertain the viability of your business. While you need a business plan when starting your brokerage firm, you can also revise it and write a new one once your operation is running.

For a start-up like yours, a business plan is a necessary document because it gives you direction. An elaborate business plan should tell someone how you plan to handle the financial, marketing and operational tasks. Other than that, it should give an accurate description of the business, the services that you offer, and how you intend to achieve your objectives.

When writing the plan, make sure you include a section on the industry overview. Investors have their own assessment of the industry and would like to compare your assessment with theirs. Usually, if you are both on the same page, it is easier to convince them to come on board. Besides the comparative concept of the industry analysis, you also must highlight the nature of competition in the segment you are investing in and how you plan to differentiate yourself while adding value to the end-users.

It is quite unfortunate that many small business owners ignore the business plan when setting up their venture. This is an important document that influences your brokerage business's beginning, growth, and sustained development over the years, so take your time and create a good one.

Value and Importance of Having a Business Plan

Financing your operation through loans or luring investors is not the only reason you should have a business plan. As a business owner, this simple document offers more value to you than you might realize. All the stakeholders in your venture have something to gain from the business plan.

Take note that your business plan does not necessarily have to be elaborate. It should be a simple document that captures the true state and nature of your business. On the same note, it should be simple enough that you can review it from time to time and update it as your operation grows. Below, we will highlight some of the benefits of having a business plan, and in the process, you will realize how valuable this document is:

1. **Business overview**

A good business plan should give you a complete overview of your operation. Each aspect of your business is interconnected. For example, from your strategic plan, someone should be able to see how your marketing plan is connected to achieving your business goals. The same applies to your sales. There should be a direct relationship between your marketing expenditure and sales. Essentially, a glimpse at the business plan should give you a bigger picture of the business.

Other than an overview of your business, the plan should also help you to identify and maintain your identity throughout the operation. Business identity is about your target market, the unique brokerage services that you offer and so on. This guides you along the way if you ever need a reality check on the nature of your business.

2. Clear priorities

Running your brokerage firm as a sole proprietor, everything rests on your shoulder. It is easy to get swamped in all that's going on around you. However, the business plan is a reminder that you cannot do everything at the same time. You can run the business and handle everything on your own, but you must have clear priorities to succeed. Through the business plan, you keep track of all the important procedures and activities. In essence, it helps you manage your effort, time, and other resources accordingly.

3. Change management

A proper business plan is necessary to help you make the required adjustments to your business from time to time. It keeps you in check. New developments, progress tracking, and frequent reviews are necessary to help you adjust your business process according to your customer's needs and the industry demands. More often, you will go back to your actual vs. plan analysis and make changes relevant to the prevailing conditions. Your business plan reminds you of your business's overall objectives, such that even with the changes made, you still stay on course towards realizing the business goals.

4. Accountability

The business plan holds you accountable for all your actions. It spells out the expectations of running the brokerage firm. A successful business is a result-oriented business. You will use the business plan for regular reviews to ensure that you are still on course. Note that challenges and disappointments are normal in business, and it is in such moments that you can look to your business plan and review progress so far. When the outlook seems fuzzy, the plan is a reminder of where you need to be.

5. Money management

For someone running their first business, it is easy to get caught up in the allure of cash flows. Seeing the profits streaming in is a good feeling. However, business is about more than that. You must account for purchases, honor your debt obligations, ensure carriers are paid on time, and take care of petty cash purchases, among other things.

Your business's monetary position should be such that it can run on its own without requiring additional financial injection from elsewhere. If you realize that you constantly have to seek financing, yet you are operating normally, something might be amiss. For example, some customers pay after services are rendered. How many such customers do you have?

Slow-paying customers keep your money on hold, forcing you to operate on debt, which is not a good position for your business. The business plan helps you to identify such challenges and make adjustments. You can talk to such customers about adjusting their payment terms, probably introducing reminders and penalties for late payments. Everyone is in the business of making money. Do not allow customers to exert unnecessary strain on your finances. You might keep them happy and keep them over the long term, but in the process, you miss the opportunity to grow your business because your funds are tied up in their operations.

6. **Milestones**

Break down your targets into achievable milestones. Milestones are the small wins you achieve on your way to greater wins. You cannot succeed overnight. Long-term business success is achieved by small milestone wins that compound into the overall success.

Let's say your overall plan is to grow your freight brokerage firm in three years. Some of the milestones you can work around include securing contracts with some big shippers or carriers, raising a given amount of cash from business operations, or growing your presence in the region. Each time you achieve one of these milestones, you are one step closer to realizing your long-term goals. Besides, milestones give you small but visible, tangible goals that you can achieve.

7. **Metrics**

Your business plan should also include performance indicators you can frequently review to determine whether you are heading in the right direction. Performance indicators are generally in numbers, so you need to identify the critical numbers for your business. For example, the number of customers, size of debt and repayment are some of the easy picks. Going further, other metrics you can monitor include conversion rates and traffic online, the number of complaints received and so on. The business plan outlines steps you will take towards success. The metrics are proof that you are doing well or not. These are useful evaluators for any business.

Starting the brokerage firm might have been one of the biggest challenges you have taken so far, but that's not the end of it. Keeping the firm alive and steering it to growth and success is even more challenging. Ultimately, a business plan helps you to maintain a strategic focus on your objectives, and in the process, offer customers quality brokerage services.

Types of Business Plans

We have looked at the value you derive from a business plan as an essential tool in your pursuit of growth and success in the freight industry. From management guides to attracting investors, this is an important document you must prepare with a lot of care. Depending on your needs and the operation, there are different types of business plans you can create. We will look at the major categories below.

1. Start-Up Business Plans

When starting a new business, you must outline how you get from idea to concept and implementation. This is where a start-up business plan comes in handy. This type of business plan will describe your business, the kind of brokerage services you offer, the management process and an honest review of the market.

Your start-up plan is incomplete without a financial analysis. Do not just dream up numbers, do some research and find out how other brokerage firms manage their operations. Include a financial analysis that outlines your cash flow projections, expected income, sales and profit.

2. Internal Business Plans

These plans are written for an internal audience in the business. For example, you can have a business plan for the marketing department to help plan your upcoming or continued marketing efforts. Internal business plans talk about the present state of the business, profitability, operating costs, etc. From this plan, you come up with strategies on how to raise or repay the capital. Ideally, this plan is pegged on the general market size, the level of influence you have on the market, and how this affects your income.

Under this category, we also have an operational business plan. This is another internal plan that addresses the factors critical to your operation. More importantly, this plan highlights your targets, deadlines and markers for the business calendar year. This is also the plan that discusses the roles and responsibilities of all members of your firm.

3. Strategic Business Plans

Strategic plans are geared towards the overall growth of the business. They highlight your goals for the freight brokerage business and how you can achieve them. Strategy formulation is key to business success because it lays the foundation for everything you will do. The outline and format of a strategic business plan vary from one business to the next, but they must all discuss the following:

- Your vision

- Mission statement

- Key success factors

- How to meet your objectives

- Implementation schedule

The main objective of strategy formulation is to shed light on each level or department's roles in your business and their contribution towards your ultimate goals. It can also present that rallying call for your team members to pull their weight and work towards the business goals.

4. **Feasibility Business Plans**

Feasibility reports the possibility of success in your brokerage venture. This is done by determining the market for your brokerage services and whether you can profit from the venture. This plan analyzes the need for your services in the market, your target audience, and the capital needed to meet those objectives. This plan is not limited to these metrics. Anything that helps you gauge the market readiness for your business's services and profitability can make it to the feasibility business plan. The metrics culminate into recommendations on how to penetrate the market and make a profit.

5. **Growth Business Plans**

As the name suggests, this plan takes a futuristic approach to the business. It is about growth projections, and for varying reasons, you prepare it for both internal and external use. Let's say you seek capital injection into the business. Your growth plan must show prospective investors a complete description of your company, the staff and management. Investors need to understand your growth plan.

You start by highlighting the targets you set for your business and show how the current business setup will help you realize that plan. You can also include revenue and expense estimates. From your projections, a growth-minded business should have enough money to stay afloat after paying all business expenses and any other financial obligations.

Lean Business Plan

As the name suggests, a lean business plan includes only the essential things your business needs. This is a watered-down version of the general business plan we have discussed in this chapter. The lean business plan is geared towards addressing the core functions of the business. Therefore, it is scanty on descriptions and is often presented to lenders and investors to give them a quick glance at the business and its position. Lean business plans are prepared for management optimization.

The lean business plan is essentially the only business plan you will ever need. Do not hurry to create a formal and lengthy business plan. It is advisable to start lean, and as the business grows, you can update the plan to reflect the new position. Below are the features of a lean business plan:

1. Strategy

A small business is easier to manage than a large business. This is because you have a bird's eye view of everything that goes on. Keep this in mind when writing the business. The smaller the business, the easier it is to avoid distractions. When writing this plan, strategy formulation is as simple as noting down bullet points. They act as quick reminders of what needs to be done and how to go about it.

The thing about strategy formulation is that it will guide all your effort going forward. Do not make the mistake of working outside the strategy plan. You will waste resources you might never recover. For strategy formulation, first figure out your business identity. This stays with you for as long as the business is in operation. Next, think about your customers and, finally, the product or service you are offering.

2. Tactics

Building on strategy formulation, work on the tactics. The strategy will still influence the approaches you use to achieve your goals. You know what your business is about and what you cannot do. You also know the target audience, so from here, come up with an action plan on how to bring the strategies to life. It is at this stage that you think about executing the business plan.

There are many tactics you can think about. Let's take marketing, for example. Consider things like the positioning of your message, service pricing, target market, how to differentiate your business from everyone else in an industry that is saturated with brokers. How will you handle sales? How do you blend traditional and effective marketing approaches with modern marketing tactics to get the best returns?

Next, you think about the product or service you are offering. How do you introduce it into the market? Are you planning a launch? Is the launch date good enough? Do you need a website, vendors, or a different delivery option when launching the business?

Everything in your business depends on the money. How are your financial plans? Do you have a good working relationship with your bank? Can they extend you a line of credit to take care of your obligations?

Note that the responses to these questions will be guided by strategy formulation. By now, you can see how interconnected every aspect of a lean business plan is. This means that you should think through all the factors involved before committing to anything. The purpose of a lean business is to limit wastage.

3. Assumptions, Milestones, Metrics, and Schedule

Once you write down the tactics, go over them again. In this section, you will add specifics to the tactics so that your effort can come to fruition. An effective plan for your tactics should have deadlines and other specifics that make them tangible.

First, work on a review schedule. This is important because things hardly go according to plan. You can remember the number of times you have had to go back on some plan because something changed. The same applies in business, especially where money is involved. You must schedule a review at regular intervals to keep up with the progress and growth in the business. If you foresee something will not happen as planned, reorganize it as appropriate.

You will make some assumptions when creating a lean business plan. Note them down on a list so that they are easier to review whenever you need to. Once the plan is in motion, track and review the results, and if they are not similar to your plan, which is most often the case, go back to the list of assumptions and identify what might have changed.

When working with assumptions, you hope that things will go according to plan, but this is not always the case. Once you identify the changes, revise the plan and monitor progress thereon for future review. Even as you look at the assumptions, you must also check to ensure that your plan was properly executed.

Milestones are about accountability. What activities must be completed by a certain time, and more importantly, who is responsible for them? Milestones help keep you in check and break down big tasks into smaller chunks that are easier to handle. They act as reminders, commitments that will get you closer to realizing your goal. Some of the milestones you can have in this case include the start and end dates, when to review budgets, and so on. This is the first point at which your management skills are called into accountability.

Finally, you have to look at the key metrics in your business. These are the performance yardsticks that inform you whether you are doing well or not. Metrics also help in management accountability. At this point, you will be looking at things like expenses, costs, and sales. If you have a website for your brokerage firm, the metrics you can consider include website traffic, referrals, conversion rates, tweets, impressions, and likes. There is an endless list of things you can consider, so try to tailor the factors to suit your brokerage business.

4. Forecasts of Sales, Costs, Expenses, and Cash

To keep the business running, you must be able to monitor and manage the money. Planning for the money helps you to make projections for the future based on current events. Without forecasting, it is impossible to track pertinent problems, results or capitalize on situations that put you at an advantage in the market.

You don't have to overthink the forecast. Since you are starting a small business, a simple forecast of costs and sales is good enough. It does not have to be accurate either, but it should be realistic so that you work within an acceptable business range.

With forecasting, you will be wrong most of the time when you look at the actual results, and this is okay. The lesson here is to review the results and identify how far your assumptions were from the real outcome. With time and experience, you will realize that your assumptions and real results are relatively close, which is a sign that you have a good grasp of the business's key factors.

With forecasting, you also have to make projections for cash flow. You cannot run the business without the money. The emphasis here is mostly about running a profitable business. Simply put, try to keep your expenses lower than your costs. The challenge most businesses face, and which you will come to realize soon enough in the freight brokerage industry, is that you usually don't get paid on the exact date you expected. At the same time, you cannot wait until you have money before you can make purchases. Therefore, the fact that you have money in the bank is not a guarantee that your business is making profits.

Freight Broker Business Plan Template

The outline below is a simple template that you can use to create a freight brokerage firm's business plan. Having looked at a lean business plan before, note that you do not have to include everything in this plan from the onset. However, as the business grows, you can update your plan with respect to the growth trajectory.

A. Executive Summary

Skip this section and write it once you complete the entire plan. It should be an overview of your business, addressing the what, why and how you will succeed. It is the highlight of your company and a crucial section if you pitch the business idea to investors.

B. Business Description and Vision

This section captures the intricate details of your freight business. When someone goes through your business plan, they should understand your core values. This is also where you introduce the growth potential of your business.

1. Mission Statement

2. Company Vision

3. Business Goals and Objectives

4. Brief Background History

C. Definition of the Market

To define your market, think about the niche you want to serve, how to reach your customers, and your projections in terms of expanding your reach. Fill this section by addressing the following aspects:

1. Industry and industry prospects

2. Potential market share

3. Target market segments

4. Target customers

5. Customer challenges and needs you are addressing

6. Key competitor profiles

D. Description of Services

The freight business is a service-centered business, which gives you a lot of room to differentiate your services from other brokers in the market. This section gives the investor confidence because they understand what your business is about, why you are in it, your competitive edge, and its value proposition. Under this section, you will discuss the following:

1. Description of Services

2. Pricing Strategy

3. Competitive Advantage

E. Strategic Direction

This section is about the SWOT analysis for your brokerage business. Analyze your business in the context of the market and industry in general. You can also propose services you plan to introduce in the future. You will discuss the following:

1. Strengths of the Freight Brokerage Firm

2. Weaknesses

3. Opportunities in the Marketplace

4. Threats

5. Future Growth Prospects

F. Marketing and Sales Strategy

In this section, you describe how you intend to grow and market the business. You will talk about the different marketing forms you plan to use, sales and advertising strategies, public relations, and promotions where applicable. You will also mention who your market is, and how to reach customers. Ensure you highlight how to make your business competitive, given the nature of competition in the industry. In this section, you will discuss the following:

1. Market Description

2. Service Demand

3. Marketing Strategy

4. Promotions Strategy

5. Sales Strategy

6. Internet Marketing Strategy

7. Strategic Alliances

G. Organization and Management

How you organize your business will determine your profitability in the market over the years. Organization management includes things like proper record keeping, accounting and billing tasks. This section informs investors of how you will run the business on a day to day basis. The outline of your business should also consider the legal status of your business. You will discuss the following in this sector:

1. Business Structure

2. Management Team and Roles

3. Organizational Structure

4. Personnel Plan, including freight agents

5. Legal Process Agents and States of Operation

6. Corporate Legal Representative

H. Financial Management

Under financial management, you should explain the numbers to your investors. This is the trickiest part of the business plan because the numbers must add up. Consider the fact that investors generally have a capable team of analysts who will vet your business plan to determine whether you are a suitable candidate for their investment.

This section should show them the expected returns so that they can make plans on how to recoup their investment. They also need to see your business's financial viability and, more importantly, your bottom line projections. Since you are just starting the business, it makes sense to work with estimates and highlight them as such. You generally have no idea what the business will look like in the foreseeable future, so it is only fair that you work with estimates. Based on your business estimates, you can prepare an income statement, balance sheet and cash flow statement.

In case you have been in the business for some time and you are probably looking for an investor to support your growth objectives, you should prepare financial reports for the past three years. If you are talking to your banker, the loan managers would be interested in looking at your personal financial statements. This gives them a better picture of the person behind the business. It is more or less their way of conducting a lifestyle audit on you. It helps them determine whether you can run a successful business or use proceeds from the business to furnish a lavish lifestyle, rendering you an unworthy candidate for their financial support.

Going through the business plan, you realize how crucial it is to think rationally and discipline yourself when managing the business. The hard work does not end at writing the business plan, either. For your business to succeed, you must follow through and review input and results from time to time.

Chapter 6
How to Find Carriers and Shippers

The next step in your business growth plan is to find regular shippers and carriers. This is the point where your business strategies come into effect. A steady flow of customers is every freight broker's dream, and to achieve that, you need to network and establish quality connections and relationships. Such relationships are built on trust and reliability, so even if you bring in a customer for the first transaction, treat them well to keep them around for the long haul.

While good marketing strategies will work for you, bad marketing is just as effective in chasing customers away. Therefore, before you get started on the strategy we will discuss in this section, you must make sure you have your marketing and communications strategies on point. For example, many first-time customers will check out your website. This is where you hit or miss. Keep things professional. You are a brand now, so try to operate your business as such.

Think of your perception when you interact with a company for the first time. The red flags you look for are the same things your customers are looking for to protect their investment. Have a professional website, logo and anything else that gives customers the best first impression of your brand. Ensure your social media pages align with the context on your website.

At any given point in time, many moving pieces in the logistics industry align to ensure that shippers, carriers and brokers move cargo from one point to another. Shippers rely on your expertise and experience in logistics, while on the other hand, you can choose those who meet the shippers' needs from your database of carriers.

You are the oil that keeps the wheels turning in this industry, and you must always act fast. So, how do you find the right carrier to move cargo for your customers? Let's look at some of the most reliable methods brokers have used over the years:

1. Referrals and recommendations

In this industry, your best customers are your best brand ambassadors. You are likely to get more leads from their business associates, friends and family members. When customers enjoy your services, they spread the word. Do not be afraid to ask them for referrals. Apart from that, establish a warm connection with them beyond the business. That way, you can use their name in your pitch to new customers for relevance and credibility. Apart from that, if your new prospects call your main customer, they will receive nothing but good words about your work. You can also reward customers for referrals.

2. Warm calling

People don't like cold calling, as much as it has worked for many businesses in the past. Imagine a company calling you out of the blue, pitching their business to you. Cold calls are often frowned upon because they are an inconvenience to the recipient, among other reasons. Instead of cold calling, why don't you try warm calling?

Look for a database of distributors and manufacturers in your region. Ensure the database is comprehensive, with more information about the target audience like relevant contact names and addresses, products they handle, revenues and so on. This database contains useful information about your potential customers and their immediate needs. Armed with this information, you can make that cold call, but since you know so much about them, appeal to their business needs. Offer them reliable and credible solutions. That is how you turn cold calls into successful warm calls.

3. Use reference sheets

Reference sheets contain names of company references when they sign credit applications. This is an excellent place to find shippers and carriers. From such lists, you can tell a company's profile and reputation by the number of times they are listed as references.

At the same time, you can also look towards other freight businesses in the market as your customers. There's a good chance your customers are also looking for business, so learn from them and you might find new customers by looking at similar entities in the market. Besides, since you have experience in moving freight, they might want to talk to you and discuss options.

4. **Monitor the competition**

Before they become your customers, they probably take their business to another broker, so they might not need your services. However, this should not put you down. Everyone is always looking to cut costs, so recommend a free audit, without any obligation on their part. If you can beat their current freight broker's rates, they can either switch to your business or keep you on their list as a backup.

Remind the customer that you are on standby if anything ever goes wrong with their current broker. From your audit, it's also possible that you might not be at their current broker's rates and still remain profitable. That's okay because at least you will know what other brokers are charging and revise your rates accordingly.

5. **Check dormant accounts**

If you keep a list of customers you work with, identify those who used to work with you but have since gone silent. Reach out to them and find out why they moved on from you. If you had some issues, show them that you fixed them, and ask to bring them on again.

Accounts might also become dormant because the customers' primary contact had left the company, or a new company acquired the business. The customers might not be comfortable working with you because they don't know you. In this case, reach out to the former account handler and ask them to introduce the customers.

6. **Send direct mail**

One of the easiest ways of reaching out to a large target audience is through direct mail. Create a profile for shippers and carriers and purchase a list that would fit those profiles. Select those companies or individuals you wish to work with and send them an introduction letter or a postcard. This is also an excellent time to send a promotional offer.

The challenge with direct mail is that the results are not instant. You must be patient and even consider mailing the target audience once a month. Each time you send the mail, be creative and send a new letter. Apart from the mail, you should also call the potential customer for a formal introduction.

Two things might happen when you make that call. One, the customer might be interested and request further clarification. Second, they might not be interested. In the second option, ask the customer if they don't mind you checking in with them from time to time, hoping that they might change their mind. Alternatively, you can also ask them to suggest an appropriate time to reach out in the future.

The concept of direct mailing is to make the customer think of you if they ever need freight brokerage services. This is why you see companies sending cards and other kinds of mail during holidays, wishing customers prosperity and happiness.

7. **Build lasting relationships**

The transport industry is purely a relationship business. To succeed as a broker, you need to create solid relationships, not just with carriers but also with shippers and consignees.

Remember that the aim is not only to get carriers to move cargo for you; you need to understand their business. You need to understand their values, too. Go beyond the corporate values and know them better.

Most carriers own fleets of trucks, so the challenge is to align your personal values with theirs. The idea here is to try and understand how they grew to where they are today. What values have kept them in the industry for so long? Besides, carriers are always in talks with each other, so you can rest assured that you will be a subject of discussion with a good relationship from time to time.

8. **Generate leads from everyday products**

Look around you. All the products you use were once delivered by trucks: Carriers transported cars, furniture, the laptop, or phone you are using right now. You can find carriers using this analogy. First, you need to find out where products used frequently around you were manufactured and how they move from the manufacturing plant to the end-user.

Another way to go about this is thinking about your most recent purchases. Try and track down the bill of lading and any other useful shipping information and documents. This should give you the names of carriers. You will have successfully created a database of local carriers that you can work with. Find out how they run their business, how far they can go, and from there, you can consider using their experience and expertise in the field to expand your brokerage firm.

9. **Online search**

Having an online presence is something every business is thinking about today. You probably have this written down in your business plan. Many carriers are embracing this concept and are getting websites and active social media pages. Unfortunately, the uptake is relatively slow, especially since most carriers operate as independent contractors or small businesses; hence, complete disregard for the benefits of integrating technology into their business operations. A quick online search for carriers in your region will be useful. Apart from that, you can also see their reviews online.

10. **Understand the freight**

It is easier to convince carriers to haul cargo for you when you both understand the contents and any unique requirements for it. Some carriers are strict on the kind of cargo they can haul, either because of personal reasons or their equipment can only allow them to handle that limit. You have an easier time getting a carrier onboard if you can describe the freight properly.

To do this, ensure the shipper gives you all the information you need. This will also make it easier to qualify carriers for cargo faster. Whenever you have urgent or crucial freight coming in, you are certain about the carriers who are comfortable transporting it and on time. You will also have a shortlist of carriers with the most competitive rates and those who can transport fragile cargo.

11. **Mastering upload settings**

Before you look for carriers, you need to understand how uploads are handled. Carriers do not like being stranded, waiting for days for cargo to be prepared. Each day the truck is not hauling cargo, they lose money. For this reason, ensure you can organize quick turnarounds before getting a carrier, such that when you contact them, the load is all set and ready to move.

12. **Consider other modes of transportation**

The transport industry is not limited to truckload carrier services. While this is common, there are other options, like rail and air freight too. Keeping your options open, you can also try and establish relations with carriers in those avenues.

Eventually, your success in this industry will come down to how well you can coordinate the needs and requirements of carriers, shippers and consignees. This is an industry where critical cargo comes up from time to time, so you must also learn to respond to them quickly.

By offering multiple ways of moving freight, you give customers more options, which translates to price flexibility from one point. Besides, when you offer these and other services, customers believe you are a growth-oriented broker, which means an opportunity to grow with your business. This way, your customers can take advantage of the opportunity to use intermodal conversion methods, saving more in the process. They can use more capacity in one mode when other modes are at full capacity.

What Do Customers Look For?

Now that we know how to find shippers and carriers, how do you keep them on your books for a long time? There are small and large brokerage firms in the market, and they all angle for the same pool of customers all the time. You can only offer quality brokerage services when you understand the needs of your customers. With this in mind, we will look at the factors that influence the customers' decisions and what they look for in a broker. This can become a checklist that helps you make sure you can meet the customer's needs.

Shippers use freight brokers for these key reasons:

1. **Capacity building** - this way, they don't need to add carriers to their routing schedule. They bring you onboard to simplify their routing schedule. In the process, you ease pressure on their routing schedule such that the shipper can handle more demand without having to expand their routing schedule.

2. **Ease of transportation** - you become an extension of their managed transportation services, streamlining the link between the logistics service provider and the shipper.

Bearing these in mind, the following are some of the things that shippers hope to find before they bring their business to you:

1. **Fully licensed broker**

You must have the required licenses to operate in the freight industry. From time to time, you will come across people purporting to offer brokerage services when, in the real sense, they do not have the necessary licenses. Do not take shortcuts. Ensure you are licensed by FMCSA (customers can verify your license online).

2. Stable finances

Shippers are interested in your financial standing to gauge whether you have the capacity to do business with them. No matter how long you have been in the industry, brokers come and go, and each time a broker winds up operations, shippers are left stranded and have to incur the costs and inconveniences of looking for a new broker.

Financial stability is also important to the shipper because if you ever close down, they bear the burden of paying carriers for the load delivered. This situation introduces the risk of double payment, including attorney fees where applicable. This is why shippers will run a credit check to ensure you are capable of handling their business.

Building on that, shippers also check to ensure you have the right insurance policies instead of their business operation. In particular, they look for contingent cargo and shipper's interest policies. The shipper's interest policy, for example, covers the cargo being transported, which is critical to safeguarding the shipper's business interests. Note that shippers can also verify whether your insurance payments are up to date.

3. Deductible

Depending on the nature of the shipper's cargo, some deductibles can be too high such that small brokers cannot comfortably handle them. Let's assume you just started your brokerage business. Processing deductibles of $30,000 would be a tall order, especially if your bank cannot assist.

4. **Vetting carriers**

Shippers are also interested in finding out how you vet carriers. This is important because you are just the intermediary. Ideally, the carriers you choose work for the shipper. Some of the industry's biggest brokers have thousands of carriers on contract, and they have a way of monitoring them.

Some of the issues shippers will need assurances about include the number of approved and active shippers you have on contract, your approval process, whether they are insured, how you monitor and update changes to the carrier profiles and how frequently you do that.

How do you confirm carrier safety ratings? Do you have a policy in place for delisting carriers who breach your terms of engagement?

5. **Reputation matters**

Reputation is vital in this industry. Even if you are a new broker, you can create a buzz around your name. Network with, and get other experienced brokers to vouch for you. When customers are looking for a broker to handle their cargo, they come with the mindset of adding an employee to their company. This is where your reputation comes in.

One way of raising your profile is to join relevant trade associations. All the major brokers in the market belong to trade associations, so some customers take it as a red flag if you do not belong to any of them. Membership to these organizations carries some weight because of their vetting procedure. Before admission, they run background checks to determine whether you are fit to become a member. From there, you can engage in their activities and even use their logo on your website. The following are some of the associations you can join, which will boost your reputation:

- Intermodal Association of North America (IANA)

- Transportation Intermediaries Association (TIA)

Most customers will check your name on the association websites. This helps them determine your credibility, especially since some rogue brokers have association logos on their websites, yet they are not members.

6. **Business footprint**

Finally, shippers will always want to see your business footprint. These days, there is so much information you can search online about a business. Their contacts, address, business history, ratings and reviews are all available online. If you have a social media page, that's one of the first places customers will check.

Customers are skeptical of brokers who do not have an online presence. If you do not have the resources to set up a website or professional company emails, for example, it hurts your reputation. If you have a website, LinkedIn and other social media pages, make sure they are professionally done and managed. From your social media and blog posts, customers have an idea of your values and beliefs. If they align with how they run their businesses, you can expect they will reach out.

Now that you know what customers look for when they need brokerage services and how to find reliable shippers and carriers, try and implement the tips in your work and see your brokerage business grow from strength to strength.

Creating Quality Brokerage Business

To succeed in the brokerage business, you must create value and offer quality services. Think of the struggle you go through to bring new shippers on board and how much effort you put into finding the right carriers for their goods. You have to find ways of keeping customers happy so that your business can grow. Unhappy customers effectively damage your brand reputation, while happy customers recommend your brokerage services. Remember that bad news travels faster than good news and usually has a lasting impact on your business.

To create a quality business in the industry, whether you are a start-up broker or have been in the business for a while, you must first tap into all the networks you have for connections. The easiest way to get a reliable carrier for a shipment is to go through your database. Keep records for all the carriers you work with and note down any significant features about their services. This will reduce the duration of time you spend looking for carriers, especially when you have urgent cargo.

Organizations like the TIA are another place you can go for carrier connections. Apart from connections, you can also use this as an opportunity to learn best practices in the market, build relationships, and make use of resources available to brokers and shippers. Once you are a member of the TIA, you have access to amazing tools that can help you streamline the carrier selection process. Membership to this body also gives you access to a list of carriers who have since been flagged for fraudulent deeds. This can help you avoid losses by contracting an irresponsible carrier.

- **Load prices and carrier quality**

For quality business in this market, you get as much as you give. This is a principle that, in utmost good faith, encourages you to operate your brokerage business as diligently as you can. One of your objectives is probably to save as much as possible from the margins in terms of costs. Remember that every other party in the industry worries about margins, too. Do not let this cloud your judgment. If all you offer are low-paying loads, you can forget about getting high-quality carriers.

In this industry, word goes around so fast, and if you have a reputation for paying carriers too little, such a reputation will stay with you for a long time. The solution is to research and understand the prevailing market rate for different load types and offer carriers rates that are reasonable and acceptable within the market. Note that the freight brokerage business prices vary from time to time, so you must also revise your load rates accordingly.

Occasionally, you will come across some low-quality drivers working with some of the industry's top carrier companies. These are random outlier situations that are expected in any market. However, you can mitigate this risk by using load schedulers that verify their carrier credentials from time to time. Alternatively, you can also seek information from insurance service providers, the licensing authorities and check their safety scores.

- **Champion the change you want**

If you want to attract the best drivers in the market, you must also have a reputation for being a responsible and reliable broker. Give your drivers the same attention and care you would expect them to give you and your customers. If you conduct business with them in a logical and ethical manner, they will return the favor.

Unfortunately, many brokers mistreat carriers, yet they expect the carriers to treat them with respect. Think about the way you conduct business. Pay carriers on time, communicate instructions to them clearly, and talk to them with respect. If you make a commitment with a carrier, follow through on it. These are some of the incentives that make carriers look forward to working with you.

That being said, you should also go the extra mile and learn about the underlying rules of the transportation and transport industry. Just because you connect a carrier to the shipper does not mean that you make them work like slaves for you. To be precise, go through the Hours of Service (HOS) regulations. This shows you the maximum number of hours a trucker should be driving, the recommended break limits, and the drivers' required sleep. Carriers haul so much dollar value in their trucks, and the last thing you want is loss from accidents because of a fatigued driver.

Besides, if you keep pushing carriers to work beyond the recommended hours contrary to the HOS regulations, you will soon find yourself on the wrong side of the law, and this might even cost you your license. As much as you want the cargo to arrive on time, it is also your responsibility to give the driver ample resources to protect other passengers and road users. Go through the delivery schedule and deadlines keenly and understand the requirements so that you do not assign carriers impossible delivery schedules. Not only will they struggle to meet those deadlines, but you also risk losing the customer because you committed to an impossible schedule. Yet, you could have easily discussed it with them and rescheduled the delivery accordingly.

- **Trust and reliability**

Be an honest freight broker. Brokers in every industry are often treated with contempt because people see the worst traits of middlemen in them. Indeed, you cannot miss a few rotten apples in every industry. You should, however, set yourself aside and abide by a strict code of conduct. For example, do not double broker a carrier.

Double brokering is a situation where the carrier, who might also be a freight broker, agrees to transport a load from another broker. Unknown to the legitimate broker, the carrier then brokers the load to another carrier. This is an illegal practice. Be as transparent as possible when conducting business with carriers and shippers. Engaging in illegal practices like double brokerage will only leave you knee-deep in legal disputes. At the same time, you earn a reputation in the eyes of shippers and carriers as an untrustworthy and unreliable broker. Such a reputation is hard to shake off.

Those who engage in such activities usually have some cash flow problems they try to overcome by circumventing the rules. Suppose you find yourself in such a position. In that case, there are many financial service providers you can work with who will offer accounts receivable products and handle carrier payments on your behalf.

Chapter 7
The Legalities and Formalities

As an intermediary, you handle shipments across state lines and, for that reason, all the broker authority businesses are operated under the purview of the FMCSA. At this point, you already know the prerequisites to become a freight broker, from obtaining your operating license to getting a surety bond and so on. The next step is to understand the legal status of your business. Away from the daily activities that keep you in business, there are legal requirements that you must meet to operate legally. Compliance is mandatory, without which you risk losing business, heavy fines, or even jail term.

Before you start your brokerage firm, you must decide the type of business entity you wish to establish. This is important because when you register the business, it becomes a separate legal entity from yourself. As a separate legal entity, your business assumes an identity as a person, such that it can sue and be sued, enter into contracts with other parties and so on.

There are different business models under which you can register your brokerage firm. Knowledge of each of them helps you determine the most suitable for your business. This is important because the type of business you register determines how you file tax returns. The last thing you want is the IRS on your case. Let's look at the common types of business under which you can register your brokerage firm below:

Sole Proprietorship

In this structure, you are the owner of an unincorporated brokerage firm. You pay personal income tax on all the profits earned from your brokerage firm. This is one of the easiest businesses to register and operate because there are no regulations. Since you don't necessarily need a separate trade or business name, many sole proprietors operate under their own names. As your business grows, however, you can convert the sole proprietorship to an LLC.

The main difference between a sole proprietorship and a corporation is that you do not create a separate legal entity. For this reason, you are responsible for all liabilities incurred and lawsuits entered into by the business. This means that your brokerage firm's debts and obligations are your personal responsibility, too.

Ease of creation, low cost of registration and maintenance, and the pass-through advantage make sole proprietorship a good option for a startup. That being said, you will usually have to raise startup capital on your own. Besides, it is not easy to get financing from established financiers like banks or obtain a credit line. There is also an unlimited liability, which leaves your personal affairs exposed if you cannot honor your business liabilities and debts. Many businesses start as sole proprietors, but you can transition into a limited liability entity as they grow.

For the purpose of taxation, where applicable, you might be liable for income tax, self-employment tax, estimated tax, social security and medicare taxes, withholding tax, federal unemployment tax, excise tax, and file information returns if you made payments in the course of your operation to non-employees.

Partnerships

A partnership is an agreement between two or more people to operate and manage a business, sharing profits in the process. There are many partnership agreements under which you can register your brokerage firm. In business partnerships, profits and liabilities are shared among the partners equally or under any other sharing agreement entered into by the partners. This is true in partnerships where some partners have limited liability. There are three main types of partnerships you can enter into:

1. General partnership

2. Limited partnership

3. Limited liability partnership

In a general partnership, everyone shares profits and liabilities equally. All partners are personally liable for the debts and obligations entered into by the partnership. Profits and losses are shared equally or according to instructions spelled out in the partnership agreement.

Professionals commonly enter into limited liability partnerships. These include doctors, lawyers, architects and accountants. The nature of their limited liability is such that if one of the partners incurs legal damages for malpractice or any other reason, the other partners' assets are not affected.

Limited partnerships are a blend of general partnerships and limited liability partnerships. In this operation, you must have at least one general partner. This partner assumes full personal liability for the debts of the partnership. You must also have at least one silent partner whose liability is limited to the amount they invested, but they do not take part in the partnership's active running.

You must file an annual information return reporting your income, deductions, profits and losses from running the freight business. However, according to the Internal Revenue Code (Chapter 1, subchapter K), instead of paying income tax, partnerships share the profits or losses among partners, who in turn report their share on their personal tax returns.

That being said, if you operate the freight business as a partnership, you might file the following forms:

1. Annual return of partnership income
2. Employment taxes including social security and medicare taxes
3. Excise tax

On the other hand, the individuals who make up the partnership might file the following forms:

1. Income tax
2. Self-employment tax
3. Estimated tax
4. International tax

For taxation, partners in a partnership are not considered employees, hence the self-employment tax. On the same note, if you want to register a freight brokerage, it might be better to register as a partnership instead of a corporation because of favorable tax obligations. For example, profits earned in corporations and dividends paid to shareholders are taxed. This is pretty much double taxation. This does not happen to partnership profits.

Corporations

Corporations are legal entities, distinct and separate from the owners. The entity registered as a corporation assumes all the rights and responsibilities that you have as an individual. This means that they can give and receive loans, sue and be sued, enter contracts, own property and other assets, pay taxes, and hire employees. Legally, a corporation becomes a person.

One of the highlights of corporations is that their liability is limited. With this, shareholders earn profits paid through stock appreciation and dividends but cannot be held liable for the entity's debts. This is the most important feature of corporations.

This entity is created by shareholders, with common stock working towards common goals. Your corporation can have one or more shareholders, depending on the nature of the business.

Corporations deduct taxable income in the same way that sole proprietors do. However, the corporation can also get special deductions. Corporation profits are taxed when the business earns them. The profits are also taxed when shareholders receive them as dividends. This is what we mentioned earlier as double taxation.

S Corporations

S corporations are also referred to as S subchapter entities. This is a special type of corporation that is set up based on unique Internal Revenue Code laws. Under this guide, if you set up the brokerage firm as an S corporation with less than 100 shareholders, you enjoy all the benefits of incorporation but get taxed as a partnership. Therefore, instead of suffering double taxation, S corporations can pass income to shareholders in the same way partnerships do.

Since all the profits, losses, credits and deductions are passed to shareholders, they are reported in their personal tax returns and assessed at income tax rates. However, S corporations are still liable for taxes on passive income. To register your brokerage firm as an S corporation, you must meet the following conditions:

1. Register as a domestic corporation

2. Have 100 shareholders or less

3. All shareholders own only one class of stock.

4. The corporation must not have been registered as any of the corporations ineligible to operate as an S corporation, such as insurance companies and financial institutions.

Once you register your company, you might only be liable to pay income tax, employment taxes, excise taxes and estimated tax. Registering your firm as an S corporation gives it credibility, especially with suppliers, potential customers and other investors because of the nature of the commitment to the business.

Since it passes taxables to shareholders, you save a lot of money that would have otherwise gone to corporate tax. Such savings are useful to startups because you can divert them to other critical aspects of the business like marketing.

For all the benefits, you must be careful when registering your brokerage firm as an S corporation. The IRS takes a particular interest in these firms because some entities try to avoid payroll taxes by disguising salaries as distributions to shareholders.

Limited Liability Company (LLC)

This is a business structure whose owners are not liable for the company's liabilities or debts. An LLC is basically a crossbreed of a corporation and a sole proprietorship or partnership. The limited liability clause of an LLC is similar to that of a corporation, but at the same time, the shareholders are taxed in the flow-through manner that happens in partnerships. Since LLCs are registered under state statutes, there might be different requirements in your state, so you should always check the requirements with the state.

Owners in an LLC are referred to as members, and unlike S corporations, there is no restriction on membership. Therefore, you can have corporations, individuals, foreign entities, or even other LLCs as members of your brokerage LLC. On the same note, while S corporation membership is capped at 100, LLCs membership is unlimited. You can also register your brokerage LLC as a single-member in many states if you wish to remain the sole owner.

For the purpose of taxation, the IRS treats your LLC as a partnership, corporation or a disregarded entity as part of your tax returns, depending on the options you choose when registering the company.

Other than the liability protection, which is the main reason business owners register companies, LLCs are easier to set up than corporations and allow you more flexibility. However, note that if you do not honor your legal requirements as an LLC or if there's proof of fraud, creditors can come after individual LLC members. Depending on the state laws applicable in your jurisdiction, you can dissolve the LLC if one of the members is dead or declared bankrupt. This is different from corporations, which exist in perpetuity.

Registering Your Business

Having looked at the different business structures, you can then move on to register your business accordingly. Choosing an appropriate business structure is essential because it will determine how you file tax returns and how much tax you pay. Generally, you don't want to spend so much of your earnings on taxes, so think about the business structure options, and choose the most appropriate one. If in doubt, you can always talk to an accountant or an attorney to help you evaluate your options.

1. **Application to the authorities**

Next, you will file your application with the relevant authorities. This industry's authority is the Federal Motor Carrier Safety Administration (FMCSA), a branch of the US Department of Transportation. They enforce safety regulations and oversee interstate commerce. Generally, it takes around four weeks to receive your authority once you submit the duly filled forms.

2. **Choose a process agent**

This will be the representative to whom legal papers can be addressed if anyone raises a court proceeding against you or a carrier relevant to your business. Since you handle cargo across multiple states, you must nominate a process agent in every state where you have an office or where you do business. Since it might be difficult to raise such an agent in all states, you can opt for blanket coverage to assign a process agent in all states within the country. Besides, you are in this business for growth, and in the transport and logistics industry, you will pretty much be serving the entire country.

3. **Organize a trust fund or surety bond**

We mentioned the importance of a surety bond or trust fund earlier in the book. It is a mandatory requirement for all freight brokers to protect shippers and carriers' interests in case you are unable to honor your contractual obligations. Visit your insurance agent and discuss this with them. It is through them that you can fill and file the necessary documents with the FMCSA.

4. Business registration

You must apply for the Unified Carrier Registration and pay the annual fee, which is usually in the range of $60–$80 a year.

With all these covered, you are ready to operate as a licensed freight broker. However, remember that states might have different requirements regarding the freight brokerage business. Therefore, make sure you check with state agents and authorities to ensure you have all that is required to operate in the state.

Compliance Requirements

The Code of Federal Regulations (CFR), Part 371 - Brokers of Property, spells out all the compliance requirements that freight brokers must adhere to. The general compliance requirements for brokers are as follows:

1. Maintaining transaction records

Under the CFR, you must maintain detailed records of all business transactions for at least three years. Some of the details covered by this statute include names and contact details of consignors, carriers, bill of lading, and the amount earned in return for brokerage services. These records are kept and open for review by any party to transactions involving your brokerage firm.

2. Avoid misrepresentation

You have a legal obligation not to misrepresent yourself as a carrier or offer a carrier's services when in the real sense, you are registered as a broker. All your marketing and advertising approaches must explicitly state that you offer brokerage services, not carrier services. Apart from that, you cannot offer or perform services in the industry under any other name apart from that which is duly licensed and registered with the FMCSA.

3. Carrier charges

You cannot charge carriers for services in which you have an interest in or own the cargo being hauled by the carrier. This statute also applies to situations where your business owns or is owned by a shipper, giving you legal obligations to control the cargo. On the same note, your brokerage firm cannot give or offer anything of value to shippers other than marketing materials of inexpensive value.

4. Responsible accounting

All business revenues and expenditures must be accounted for in your accounting books, especially when they are derived from other business forms other than the freight brokerage services. Revenue and expenditure related to the brokerage service should be distinct from additional revenues and expenses. In case they are shared, you must allocate them equitably.

5. **Annual bond renewal**

One of the most important compliance requirements for brokerage firms is to ensure you renew your annual bond on time. It seems like a simple thing, but considering the number of brokerage firms submitting renewals for approval, you can expect delays from time to time.

Apart from delays, you can also make the innocent mistake of forgetting to renew your bond on time, as do other freight brokers in the market. Note that the FMCSA is within its mandate to suspend your brokerage license without the renewal. To avoid this, sureties will generally send you renewal reminders 60 days before yours expires, and in some cases, earlier. To prevent unfortunate mishaps and risk losing your license, renew your bond as soon as you receive the surety's reminder. This gives them sufficient time to process the application and forward to FMCSA.

The Transportation Management System (TMS)

A transportation management system (TMS) is a logistics platform that leverages technology to enable you to plan, execute and optimize the movement of incoming and outgoing cargo. Such a system is also useful in ensuring all the carriers and cargo are compliant, and you receive all the necessary documentation regarding the undersigned shipment. By design, a TMS is an important extension of a supply chain management system.

One of the key roles of the TMS is to bring visibility to your daily brokerage operations by supporting compliance, ensuring freight is received delivered on time and streamlining the shipping process. An efficient TMS makes it easier for you to optimize and manage your brokerage business

's transportation aspect.

As an essential cog in supply chain management, they affect all logistics processes, which translates to high customer satisfaction because of efficient transport planning and execution. Satisfied customers mean more sales and business growth. The following are some of the opportunities you enjoy with a good TMS:

- Allows you to update cargo to the system

- Processes invoices

- Searches for available and relevant transport

- Real-time cargo and fuel tax tracking

- Updating cargo status

- Route planning and logistics

- Accounting

Benefits of Freight Broker Software

Given all the programs available in the market at the moment, you might be spoilt for choice. Once you know the key features to look for, you can purchase the best program to support your brokerage business. The following are some of the main benefits you will enjoy when using any of the top-rated programs in the market:

- **Shipping calculator**

A good program shows you upfront on what it costs to deliver cargo from one point to the next. This helps you plan accordingly when talking to carriers and shippers. The freight shipping calculator considers the requirements for transporting cargo from point to point, including the type of transport available and suitable for the underlying cargo, type of cargo, and conditions necessary for transport.

- **Carrier selection**

With so many carriers available at any given time, you should be able to narrow down your choices based on carrier suitability for the cargo. Some of the factors taken into consideration include the route, type and volume of cargo. A good program allows you to create filters to help you select the best carrier.

- **Benefits of consolidation**

As much as you are in the business of connecting carriers and shippers, you must also try to reduce overheads in the process. One way of doing this is to consolidate cargo where possible. You can reduce unnecessary expenses by consolidating similar items for a carrier.

- **Choosing the best route**

When choosing an ideal route for delivery, many factors come into play. Things like the fuel cost, distance, and road condition do not just determine the best route, but it also affects the delivery timeline and the cost. Good programs consider such factors and help you optimize and select the best delivery route.

- **Real-time cargo tracking**

Everyone involved in the delivery process is always at ease when they know where the cargo is at any given time as long as it is in transit. The shipper's concern is the safety of their cargo, while your concern is the carrier's safety and the delivery of the cargo. This is where real-time tracking comes in. This allows you to track cargo all the time and on any route. With updates at regular intervals, you can convey the estimated arrival time to the shipper if anything happens on the carrier's route and alert them of any emergencies or delays that are beyond yours or the carrier's control. This level of transparency will not just give the shipper peace of mind. It will also build their trust in you and your brokerage services.

Choosing the Best Software

From the benefits discussed above, you need quality brokerage software if you are to succeed in this industry and become a reliable broker. Such programs help you work faster, efficiently manage customer shipment and expectations, and in the process, earn more money by eliminating unnecessary costs.

There are two ways of going about this. You can consult a team of experts to build a TMS unique to your brokerage firm or obtain a license for one of the top programs available in the market. The first option is more expensive because developers have to build an app from scratch. It will also take more time.

Other than that, there are added costs for maintenance and updates, and since the program is unique to your business, you might struggle if you encounter bugs or problems that the developer had not factored in.

Buying a license, however, makes more sense. There is always a team of developers working round the clock to manage and maintain the program. Here are some tips to help you choose the best freight brokerage program:

- **Go for brokerage software**

There are many programs in the market, but not all of them are ideal for your business. You want something custom-made for freight brokers. Many of the programs you find are a complete bundle that includes features useful to carriers, shippers and fleets. The extra add-ons are necessary for you, but you will still pay for them.

Besides, with all the functions you don't need, the program becomes too difficult to learn, and it's even more challenging to integrate into your operation. The best option is to look for programs built explicitly for freight brokers. Alternatively, contact a software developer to create one unique to your needs, though this is generally pricier.

- **Flexible software**

You are in the business for growth. Any software you purchase for your business must support this cause, too. It is wise to look for programs whose functions can scale up as your operation grows. Apart from scaling up, it should be flexible to integrate into other services or customize it to suit your needs.

- **Data security**

The last thing you want to be vulnerable to in the business world today is a data breach, especially when you consider the nature and commercial value of the cargo you handle. Bearing this in mind, talk to an expert on proper data security and storage. You can store data on a server, offline, or with a professional service provider.

Whichever you choose, you must still conduct regular system audits to ensure your data is safe, and more importantly, follow all the guidelines necessary to protect your and your customers' data safe. Note that irresponsible data handling leading to a severe breach will not just damage customer trust in your brokerage firm. You might also suffer hefty fines and penalties.

- **Easy to understand**

Choose a program that is easy to understand. You don't want to spend a lot of money on training, especially when you scale the business and hire a team to assist you. If you are unable to understand the program, chances are high that your team might also struggle. Besides, if the program is too complicated, you might leave yourself exposed to data breaches. Apart from training, you should also purchase a product whose developers offer regular updates. You don't want to be left with a program that has not received updates in a long time or one that might be discontinued in the near future.

Top Freight Brokerage Software

While there are many programs in the market, the secret is to find one that offers features you can use immediately or in the foreseeable future. Other functions you can consider include carrier portal, management, generating quotes, database and dispatch management, scheduling and trip logs. You cannot find all these functions in one program.

Some of the functions might also be available but not work the way you expect them to. An acceptable trade-off is to find a program that meets most of your needs. Below are some of the top freight brokerage programs you can get in the market:

Aljex: Starts at $290 a month

Key features:

- You can control access and visibility to agents, protecting sensitive information
- Monitor shipment in real-time
- Monitor prices and compare with historical rates
- View dispatch on maps
- Secure cloud backups and hosting
- Easy document management and imaging
- Automated invoice payment and freight billing

Loadpilot: Starts at $99 a month

Key features:

- Integrated accounting system

- Supports international shipment handling
- Can integrate into load boards
- Job and load tracking
- Supports multimodal transportation and management

Truckstop: Starts at $ a75 month

Key features:

- You can add an unlimited number of users
- Simple invoice handling
- Easy to create a bill of lading
- Imprint your logo on all company documents
- Integrate with QuickBooks
- Supports sales management tools

3plsystems: Comes with a free demo. Full pricing upon consultation

Key features:

- Supports carrier selection
- Includes sales management tools
- Customers can track shipments on the portal
- Integrates with leading accounting suites like QuickBooks
- You can create sales quotes and track shipments to each account

AscendTMS: Starts at $69 a month, per user

Key features

- No license, setup, training, or maintenance fees
- Tech support available all-round the clock
- Free carrier and driver verification
- You can check credit scores
- Access to shipper directory
- Automated carrier payments
- Integrate into QuickBooks

Rose Rocket: Starts at $99 a month

Key features

- Minimal data entry involved
- Manage multi-carrier and multi-movement orders
- Supports LTL distribution
- Manage route and shipment expenses
- Automated invoice processing

Axon: Starts at $99 a month

Key features

- Quick invoice processing
- Receive fuel reports instantly
- Real-time integration into accounting suites
- Fleet management services

- Offers transport management services

Tailwind: Starts at $99 a month per user

Key features

- Settle driver and carrier payments instantly
- Text messaging services
- Quote and order system
- Customize your business logo
- Includes a customer and vendor database
- Payables and receivables account management
- Integrate into QuickBooks Online

Q7 Trucking Software: Starts at $20 a month

Key features

- Supports truckload and brokerage dispatch
- Fleet management
- Fuel and mileage management
- Payroll and accounting services
- Supports LTL dispatch

Logitude: Starts at $39 a month

Key features

- Freight forwarding management
- Prepare financial statements
- Automated invoice handling

- Manage shipment quotes seamlessly
- Personalization functions for all business sizes

CloudWadi: Starts at $35 a month

Key features

- Support online request handling
- Custom clearance services
- Manage accounting and prepare financial statements
- Automated invoice handling
- Includes a CRM
- Real-time cargo tracking

Logistically: Starts at $300 a month

Key features

- Manage sales online
- Supports accounting services
- Easy rate negotiation
- Support truckload and LTL management
- Customize to suit your business needs

FreightPath: Starts at $25 a month

Key features

- Scalable according to your business needs
- Easy collaboration with drivers and shippers

- Customize business documents with your color scheme and logo
- In-built invoice support

Chapter 8
Grow Your Business With Smart Marketing

You have realized, by now, how big the freight brokerage business is. As long as the world keeps spinning on its axis, cargo is always moving from one place to the other. This means that there is an endless demand, and to fulfill that demand, there will always be many freight brokers in the market. Whether or not you are new to the industry, there is plenty of fish in the sea for everyone. Essentially, the business is between the shipper and the carrier, but you are an important middleman whose services make work easier for everyone involved. With the competition in this industry, you must be sharp at marketing your services.

The industry has been transforming over the years. Today, there is so much more technology in play than there was a decade ago, which proves the evolution of freight brokerage over the years. If you are getting into the freight brokerage business today, you must think about lead generation and digitizing your enterprise.

As much as networking and connections earned through personal relationships in the industry were, and still are, useful in winning contracts, you have to do more. Connections are an excellent tool in your arsenal within this industry, but without structuring your business for modern society and the modern customer, you are bound to fail.

You must work towards finding new and more effective ways of reaching out to customers and keeping them satisfied. Large brokerage firms are taking advantage of technology to widen their market share, and if you do not follow suit and align your brokerage firm with the changing times, you stand to lose a lot. So, how do you use marketing techniques to build a resilient freight forwarding business? The answer is in lead generation.

Lead generation is a marketing process where you raise awareness and interest in your brokerage products and services. The end goal is to obtain new customers and keep the old ones happy. Lead generation makes use of digital channels for capturing, qualifying, and converting leads. To get you started, we will discuss some practical marketing methods that will get you closer to the results you yearn for.

This chapter will delve into effective marketing strategies that will help you drive sales and boost your reputation among carriers and shippers. Marketing is key to your success in this business, so devote as much time and resources as you can to it, and the results will be worth your investment. Below are useful tips to help you create quality marketing content for your freight brokerage firm:

Originality

Given the number of brokers in the market, you cannot take chances with copied content. You are selling yourself as a brand, so you must come up with original marketing material. True, you can borrow ideas from elsewhere, but the final product you present to customers should be unique and show your brand in the best light.

Regarding originality, you must also curate marketing content that is relevant to the industry. There is so much to work within this case. The industry keeps growing, and one of the areas you can shed light on is the impact of technology trends and how they shape the future of freight forwarding. Customers will not just come to you for business. They will also come to you because you seem knowledgeable and they can learn a thing or two from you.

You can also borrow from several datasets available in the market and make your own analysis. This makes for good reading on your blog if you have a website. You can also share links to your social media pages for further interaction. You might even find some of the industry's top players commenting on such content, and when such authority figures reach out, you are doing something right.

Customer-Centric Content

While the emphasis is on creating original content, you must also make sure it is geared towards the customer's needs and interests. Let's say your new target is shippers in the retail sector. There is always something new in the retail industry that you can create content around. The idea here is to keep customers interested in your content and convert that to business leads.

Another opportunity that many freight brokers miss from time to time is to leverage their marketing efforts on world events—

for example, the World Cup. Research and find out what people need in sporting retail outlets. Find out the challenges that shippers and carriers have in terms of delivering on their end of the supply chain, and address such in your marketing content. Do not just sell stories; sell a call to action. Once shippers read your blog post, for example, encourage them to get in touch for a quote to deliver their World Cup merchandise on time.

Online Marketing

Creating unique content gives you an upper hand in marketing your brokerage firm because your material becomes the springboard for all your marketing efforts. First, ensure you have a professional website. Online audiences are big on aesthetics, so you cannot take that for granted. Once you have content on your website, you can share it with the relevant parties.

From the moment you enter the industry, start building a mailing list. Keep emails of all customers you work with and add them to your email marketing list. The beauty of email marketing is that you are always in charge, and you can send customers fresh content whenever you have it ready.

Another option that many people use today is podcasting. Podcasts have recently become popular in every other niche. There is always someone running a podcast about something dear to them. You can discuss issues in-depth through podcasts and explain them better than you would have done using written content. It is about owning and controlling a narrative.

Through podcasts, you can also reach out to some of the industry's authority figures and discuss some of the current issues affecting freight brokers, carriers, and shippers. You can talk about the impact of new regulations or legislation on the bottom-line for industry stakeholders. This approach gives you credibility and raises your profile.

Finally, the mother of them all—social media. Currently, any credible business must have an online presence on social media. Twitter and LinkedIn, in particular, are great assets for businesses. You can use the platforms to engage users and drive leads to your brokerage website. You can use social media to establish relationships with customers. From your conversations, encourage them to join your email marketing list.

Understand Customer Needs

All players in the freight and logistics industry have varying needs in relation to your brokerage services. While some need customer clearance, others need reefer containers or trucking services. To market your brokerage effectively, you must understand what your customers need. This way, you can offer them a good value proposition by showing them the benefits of working with you.

To understand customers, talk to some of your current customers. Learn their purchasing process and use that to guide them towards signing up for your services. Another option is to use Google Analytics. This is a free, useful tool whose metrics offer incredible insight into your website's customer behavior and interaction.

Without facing them directly, you can also learn from competitors and understand how they keep their heads up in the industry. This can shed light on their lead generation approaches, which you can also try out.

Today, there are many discussion forums from where you can interact with all kinds of shippers, carriers, and freight brokers. In such places, you learn about their challenges, fears, and everything else in the business. Note down the complaints and do something about them. Present your brokerage business as the solution to their problems.

Understanding customer needs is key to creating a customer persona through which you can understand the ideal customer and how to reach out to them. This information will also be useful in our next point.

Create a Professional Website

It is one thing to create a website and a whole different ball game to create a professional and effective one. A professional website must deliver an incredible user experience for customers. Ideally, you want people to come to your website and spend more time on it. This is where the user experience is important. It helps you to add value to customers. People generally come to your website looking for solutions. Whether they need to move cargo or get a quote, their experience on your website should be smooth and streamlined, or they will never return.

A good user experience also helps to market your brand. It gives carriers, shippers and other users an idea of the kind of business you operate, and more importantly, gives them confidence that you can handle their freight forwarding needs.

Lead generation is essential in converting online traffic to contracts, and user experience is an integral part of that. An engaging website coupled with a well-thought-out buyer journey is the boost your marketing strategy needs.

Work on Your Content Strategy

You have come across the words SEO at some point. SEO, when done properly, will also boost your visibility online. It should be one of the elements of your content strategy. It is about planning, creating and managing engaging content. You can use SEO strategies in your infographics, videos, blogs and any other content you produce online.

Search engines appreciate SEO-friendly content and rank them well, giving you a wider reach to customers whose intention is to do business with you. You can also use different SEO tools to get insight into search keywords that customers use frequently and use those keywords to your advantage.

Even if you are new to the industry, you can learn from your competitors by analyzing their website and the keywords people use to find them, informing you of the kind of information that interests customers.

An excellent example of a content strategy that adds value is to post content about relevant news in the industry, breaking news, guides, how-to articles, or any other type of content that your customers will enjoy. Even with a good strategy, you must also make sure you produce quality content to bring customers closer to contracting you.

Market Your Strengths

Advertising your business as a freight brokerage service is not enough to convince customers to do business with you. Instead, go the extra mile and highlight the benefits of using your brokerage services. For example, one broker will offer affordable and unbeatable rates to shippers who sign up and make their first transaction in one week. This works, but it is not convincing because the user cannot quantify affordable and unbeatable value. Instead, you can offer a 30% discount to customers who sign up and make their transactions within one week. Anyone who reads the second offer will instantly do the math and tell how much they save if they use your brokerage service.

An easy way to do this is to list all the services you offer and its benefit. Note that your customers are constantly bombarded with offers as big as the market is, so be careful not to offer the same things as everyone else. Be creative and make your offers valuable.

Buyer Journey Stages

Your rates might be attractive and bring customers to your website, but what moves them from the website to your accounting books is your knowledge of the customer's journey. The first step is to ensure there are many contact points with potential customers. The customer journey is a three-step process as follows:

1. Top of the funnel - This is the stage where people seek answers through blogs, eBooks, whitepapers and any other content they find online.

2. Middle ground - In this stage, potential customers evaluate information by performing in-depth research. They review product demos, webinars, review case studies and so on.

3. Bottom of the funnel - It is at this point that you offer a lasting solution. You get customers to make a purchase. This is where you offer incentives, coupons, or free consultations.

Once you master this consumer journey process, you can gradually use it to influence the content you create and guide users progressively from the top to the bottom channel.

Call to Action (CTA)

A call to action is a subtle prompt for an immediate response from users. CTAs should be placed strategically so that they don't look out of place, or it doesn't feel like you are ambushing or coercing customers into making a decision.

CTAs help in confirming conversions. You can create an incredible blog post and attract a lot of traffic, but if, at the end of it, you do not encourage the customers to do something, that effort and attention will go to waste.

You have come across CTAs when browsing your favorite websites online. They exist in many forms, and the most effective ones usually show a popup when you do something. For example, if you were scrolling down a webpage and you suddenly go for the close (x) button, you will get a popup asking you to sign up for the newsletter or not to go away and miss a 50% discount offer.

CTAs are effective, but how you place them makes them even more useful. You can use them as hyperlinks within your content. Traditionally, most people place them in the sidebar or footer of their webpages, but these do not usually have good results. The best option is to study the market and learn the best practices for using CTAs and apply them to your website. The thing about CTAs is that there is never one method that cuts across the board. Things change all the time, and to succeed with them, you must be ready to experiment and find a good blend that complements the website UX.

Quality Landing Pages

All the marketing you engage in should lead users to a professional landing page. Once you identify the most efficient CTAs and how to work them into the website UX, cap it off with an amazing landing page. A good landing page should encourage users to subscribe to the services you offer, submit their contact information in exchange for something, message you for clarification, or request a quote.

A compelling landing page should have a convincing title, followed by a concise message about what you expect from users. If you have a submit button, it should be visible and, more importantly, if you have more than one offer, they should all have dedicated landing pages.

Perform A/B Testing

All the marketing tips above will help you make some progress in getting attention to your website. However, it does not end there. The final step is to learn how to perform A/B testing. A/B testing is simply a process of comparing two pages to identify the difference in customer engagement. It is a controlled experiment to identify outliers and understand the reason for them.

When comparing two web pages, you might realize that affect conversion rates are the different placement of the CTA buttons, the overall layout of the webpage, colors used on the page, or even media content uploaded on the site. The idea behind A/B testing is to make sure that your website is always optimized for the best results, both for your marketing needs and the customer's value proposition.

Cold Calling

Cold calling is a marketing technique that is often looked down upon by many experts in the field, yet it is still one of the most effective tactics, especially in the freight brokerage business. At some point in your brokerage career, you have had to call a stranger and tried to convince them to get something you have, which you are not sure they want.

Cold calling requires confidence and, in the freight business, you cannot do without it. You are pretty much soliciting attention and business from potential customers who were not necessarily looking forward to or expecting your call. While most of it involves calling potential customers, you can also make a surprise visit in person.

It is an incredibly effective approach for a small business whose target audience is small but well-defined. The idea is to look for paying customers for your freight business. First, you must know where to find shippers, for example, directories and shipper databases.

Establish a working profile for your target based on specific demographic units. By the time you call a customer or their company, you should have done your research on them. You should know what their business is about and some of the challenges they experience. This gives you an upper hand because you should be ready with solutions to their problems when they pick up. Cold calling is pretty much an impromptu interview.

You must be organized and ready with a script. Preparing a script helps you control the narrative and the entire conversation. This makes it easier to lead the customer and get answers to all the questions you need. Even though your script will work, you must tweak it from time to time while still delivering quality results. The conversation starters, for example, cannot be the same all the time. You might learn the hard way that it is not easy to use the same line on a shipper in New York that you used on someone in Wisconsin.

Now, before you cold call someone, you must understand that they do not expect your call. Therefore, there's a good chance that your call will be a nuisance to them. If they pick up, but you lack that confident, authoritative voice, you will lose that contact. Be keen on the hours you call and the number of times you call. You must be relaxed because some customers can tell when you are not comfortable, and your anxiety will lose you that business.

Unless you are asked to, do not try to sell the recipient anything. If they answer your call, your objective is to get them comfortable enough to talk about their challenges. This is how you gain insight into their business and the opportunities you can derive from them. If your prospect mentions something that has bugged them for a while, try and dig in deeper so that you understand the real nature of their struggles. The more you get them talking about their pain points, the more opportunities you will uncover to solve their problems.

There is always a chance that a shipper can turn things around and quiz you about your freight brokerage service, your business model, capacity and customers you currently serve. If this happens, be confident and pitch your business to them as competently as you can. If you have a good TMS program, you can track all this information and run it by the potential customer. Remind them that you have real-time tracking and can see where your transit cargo is at all times.

How do you make cold calling work for you? First, you must prepare a list of potential calls you will make. If you have been in the industry before in a different capacity, you can also start with your contact list. Since you are not new to the industry, you are in a better position to offer competitive rates because you already understand the logistics industry's ins and outs.

Another method of cutting down on costs is to optimize the destination transportation by connecting companies that might need consignments moved around the same destination. Say you are having a consignment dropped at some destination. Call them beforehand and let them know about it. At the same time, since you will have a mode of transport ready after dropping off the load, find out if they have any load to be picked. This method might not always be successful, but there are times when the company might even need to drop off their own load. By offering them the service at a discounted rate, you create a good rapport with the company. Persistence is key when dealing with such companies. They might not have something for you to move at first, but when you keep asking and offering to assist, you might get a once-off order, which is an opportunity you can turn into repeat business.

You are playing in the big leagues now, so ensure that you have a professional approach and give your brand a fitting outlook. Create professional brochures and business cards. Let people know you are starting a freight brokerage business and get your family, friends, and acquaintances to help you spread the word. All you need is a breakthrough into the industry, one contact that breaks the ice for you, and from there, you can grow your presence in the business using diligent business approaches.

Since this is a reputation and networking industry, you must also strive to make a name for yourself. Referrals from your customers always work like a charm. As long as word keeps spreading about your professional approach, individual and corporate shippers might soon start reaching out to enjoy similar benefits too.

The bottom line is that cold calling is an entirely legitimate way of trying to get business, but from time to time, the call comes in at an unexpected hour and might be a bother. Understanding the best practices for cold calling can help you go beyond these challenges. You will also come up with a logical and friendly way to contact potential customers. Cold calling is about patience, waiting until you have enough information on or from the customer before presenting your value proposition to them.

Marketing is a crucial part of the freight business. Most brokers who invest heavily in marketing generate quality traffic and from their conversion rates, they are able to improve their business models and grow. As much as you invest in different marketing approaches, you must also make sure that your business is well-positioned for the kind of transformation you are going after. This way, you will not be overwhelmed by the engagement and interaction you receive from potential customers online.

Conclusion

The market projections and economic outlook for the freight brokerage business are promising. Even in the aftermath of a global pandemic, there is so much to look forward to. As a freight broker, running a successful business means a burning desire to offer customers and business partners accurate, relevant and timely information about their business interests. In general, the industry has experienced many challenges in recent times, as has every industry in 2020. However, things are beginning to align and the growth potential for this industry is high.

Starting a business is a bold move that many people are willing to take, so the fact that you are thinking about it is a massive step in the right direction. As an entrepreneur, you learn to brace yourself for the unknown. There are many risks involved in business, but you find ways to mitigate them and navigate the turbulent tide.

This book teaches and empowers you to become not just a freight broker but an astute businessperson. Getting into the freight brokerage industry, you realize fast how close-knit the relations are, yet it is one of the world's largest industries. This is a testament to one reality—reputation is key to your success as a broker.

About reputation, you will soon realize that there are all kinds of participants in this industry. You will come across fraudulent carriers, impatient shippers, and other characters that might make you question your resolve and motivation to do business with them. Like every other business enterprise, this is nothing new. The secret is learning how to overcome such obstacles and run a profitable and credible freight brokerage business.

Just because you come across one or two people who are cutting corners and making it in the freight industry does not mean you should do the same. Unfortunately, many young entrepreneurs get into the market and are caught up in the allure of chasing quick riches. Before you know it, the law catches up, and you lose not just your good reputation, you also lose the business. You have to be patient and build your brokerage empire one brick at a time.

With all market indicators pointing towards steady growth in the brokerage industry, this is as good as any other time to set up your brokerage firm. While the global economy has slowed down in light of the coronavirus pandemic, it is worth mentioning that the freight industry is still operational. Naturally, there has been slow uptake in many parts of the world resulting in backlogs from time to time, but this is normal in the event of a global disruption of such a scale.

We comprehensively covered the requirements for setting up a freight brokerage business and with this information, you will have an easier time getting started. We also covered the market research and analysis on the freight brokerage business, highlighting the competitive advantage and the impact of disruptive technology in the market. This will give you a better head start going into the business because you already know what to do. An important highlight, in this case, is the fact that because of the technological benefits, you can now compete at the same level as some of the top brokerage firms in the industry.

Most recently, many industries have changed their mode of operation, with many sending employees to work from home. This is also a benefit you can realize in the brokerage industry. You do not necessarily have to show up at the loading docks in-person to ensure that carriers have the correct load. This can be organized from the comfort of your home. This way, you alert the carrier to pick up a consignment and deliver it to the shipper without wasting time and resources. You have more time to spend with your family and loved ones instead of spending hours on end jostling with clearing agents.

When we talk about room for growth in this industry, we are not just talking about room for brokers. Once you establish your position in the market, you can also diversify your operation and even start your trucking company. The fact that you understand the freight business better than an outsider gives you an advantage. With the network and resources available to you, it is possible to earn more when you have a registered trucking company. You can start with one truck and, with time, add more to your fleet as the business grows. That being said, you must be careful not to have a conflict of interest when managing the business.

Like most people getting into a new business, one of your concerns is probably the cost of setting up the brokerage business. We outlined the primary cost centers, and once you plan around it, you will realize that you don't need a sizable capital outlay to start. Obtain the necessary licenses, and if you do not have the funds to set up an office, you can work from home. Most of the successful freight brokers you meet in the business started with no more than a desk or working on their dining table at home. With diligence, commitment to the cause and motivation, they went on to grow their operation. As the boss, this business offers you the flexibility to move at your own pace.

If you are thinking about the future, freight brokerage is the right place for you. Success in this business can be the beginning of a huge family business, a legacy that will come for generations. This can be your opportunity to create generational wealth, making your family name one of the industry's household names. What more are you waiting for? Get started and become a freight broker today!

Through your feedback, I am encouraged to write more, which is why I would, as always, love to hear how this book helped you. As writing books is my livelihood, it would mean the world to me if you could write a review with your feedback. With that said, it is time for me to bid you farewell. I wish you the best of luck!

References

Bowen, G. (2018). Trucking company : How to start a trucking company and a freight broker business startup guide. Createspace Independent Publishing Platform.

Burton, T. T. (2016). Global KATA : Success through the Lean Business System Reference Model. Mcgraw-Hill Education.

Debaise, C., & Wall Street Journal (Firm. (2009). The Wall Street Journal complete small business guidebook. Three Rivers Press.

Fliedner, G., & Mathieson, K. (2009). Learning lean: A survey of industry lean Needs. Journal of Education for Business, 84(4), 194–199. **https://doi.org/10.3200/joeb.84.4.194-199**

Guthrie, T. B. (2007). The freight broker's handbook : ten steps to successful brokering. Guthrie Transportation Consultants.

Mccarthy, A. (2017). Freight broker business startup : How to start, run & grow a successful freight brokerage business. Valencia Publishing House, Lexington, Ky.

Mucciolo, L. (1987). Make it yours! : How to own your own business, buy a business, start a business, franchise a business. Wiley.

Серебрянская, Н. А. (2017). Intermodal freight transport models as a strategic direction in the operation of freight forwarding companies. Politechnical Student Journal, 7. https://doi.org/10.18698/2541-8009-2017-2-66

Trucking Business Startup

Step-by-Step Guide to Start, Grow and Run Your Own Trucking Company in as Little as 30 Days

Clement Harrison

Introduction

"Build your own dreams or someone else will hire you to build theirs."

- Farrah Gray

Do you fit any of the following descriptions?

- You're looking to start a home business but haven't figured out how.

- Looking for a business that you can start from home.

- Are interested in boosting your income?

- You're a truck driver tired of driving for others and want to go big and make money, plus own your time.

- You simply want to start your own business and be your own boss.

- Or you're a stay-at-home parent looking for the right business to start.

If one of the above describes you, then I have good news for you. Let me explain.

The United States has the third highest population in the world, with just over 328 million people. All these people are consumers. They are always looking for something to eat and enjoy. Entertainment is a big component of life and Americans enjoy it. Now, there's one industry that ensures that American people get the bulk of what they consume. That industry is trucking. And it currently transports over 72% of the freight in the U.S.

Why am I telling you this? The answer is simple. The trucking industry thrives because of small businesses. And you can join the bandwagon and enjoy a piece of this industry's cake worth over $700 billion. What's exciting is that anyone with the desire to get into this industry can do so because it has a low entry barrier.

So, if you've been wanting a business idea to start your venture, here's an opportunity. You may think that it's a disadvantage if you have no background in trucking. Like with anything in life, especially in the information age, it's quick to get up to speed with the right knowledge. And I'll show you in a moment what's inside this book to get started right.

In fact, people interested in starting a trucking business ask questions such as:

1. Can I start a trucking business without having to drive?

2. Is trucking a profitable business?

3. Do I need a lot of money to start a trucking business?

4. What are the risks of starting a trucking business?

5. How do I get a loan for my business?

6. Where do I find customers?

7. What permits do I need?

8. What laws should I know about?

If you have one or more of the above questions, then this book is for a person like you. As you read through the contents, you'll notice how easy it is to start a trucking company from scratch. You may not have a commercial driving license and are eager to get one, but this book covers that process.

Let me tell you what you'll learn throughout the book.

The key to winning in business is to start a business in an industry with a proven growth record. This metric assures you of ongoing business growth. With this in mind, Chapter 1 paints a clear picture of why you may be missing out on one of the best types of small businesses that you could start.

Importantly, you'll discover factors that influence the trucking business so that you can position your company for success, not failure.

Now, you may be wondering if trucking businesses are profitable. That's a legitimate concern, and I hear entrepreneurs worrying about their ventures often. It's no use running a business at a loss. You're in luck because you can operate a profitable trucking company for sure. However, you'll need to get four things right to become profitable.

New business owners often worry about start-up costs. Indeed, the trucking business requires you to have start-up capital, but you don't need to have vast amounts of cash stashed somewhere to start this kind of venture. I'll show you how to craft a business plan that improves your chances of getting funding. Above all, you'll learn the reasons behind trucking business failures. Armed with this knowledge, you'll defend yourself against the possibility of becoming a victim of business failure.

As you can guess, the trucking industry is unique. There are certain legal requirements that you'll need to meet. And they begin with ensuring that your business is legal. I'll explain the different kinds of entities that you could start, plus their pros and cons. Most importantly, this book will cover the various permits that your business needs. I do this for one reason: I want you to get started right so you can build your business on a solid foundation.

Once you have all the necessary paperwork in place, I'll take you through how to build your fleet of trucks. You'll understand the advantages and disadvantages of buying or leasing your trucks. You need the right truck ownership strategy to maximize your chances of success as a start-up. Above all, it's vital to select the right equipment for the kind of freight that you want to load and ship. Should you choose to buy your own trucks, that would be no problem at all! I'll walk you through the different financing opportunities.

A trucking business cannot succeed without good drivers. These drivers ensure that you deliver what you promise in the freight contracts. As long as you do what you say you'll do, customers will love your company, and they'll want to keep doing business with you. That's why I describe how to hire good truck drivers. Included are the criteria to look for while hiring. Most importantly, I will show you how to find the kind of customers you want for your business. This is crucial because customers bring cash to the company.

Another vital skill in business is negotiating. I've covered this so that you can use it to get high-paying freight loads and make more money.

Running a business can be intimidating if you aren't sure what and how to manage it. One vital aspect of sound business management involves managing finances. Entrepreneurs often dislike this part of the business. Hence, they mistakenly give it to bookkeepers or some accounting professionals. These experts are good at generating numbers but are not necessarily professional business managers. This is your job as a business owner.

That's why I show you the main accounting terms and financial statements so that you can be able to manage your business finances.

Not only will I show you the value of monitoring business expenses, I'll also take you behind the scenes and reveal how fuel taxes get calculated so that you can be strategic in how you buy fuel. A good fuel-buying strategy will go a long way in improving the profitability of your venture.

Perhaps you may be wondering what gives me the authority to write a book about the trucking business. It is my passion to help others succeed in life; I am a bestselling author and founder of a consultancy firm called Muze Publishing.

I come face to face with many entrepreneurs and people of all walks of life who want to free themselves from the 9 to 5. It pleases me when their lives turn for the better because of our advice. Because I focus on the fundamentals of business and personal success, my ideas are applicable in almost every industry.

What you're about to learn has helped people from many different backgrounds enjoy personal and business success.

We've helped dozens of entrepreneurs start and build successful businesses with our books. And I decided to write this book to help people like you start their own successful trucking business. There's no doubt that small businesses carry a country like ours on their shoulders. For example, the proportion of small businesses in the trucking industry is around 91%. You can imagine the impact that these small businesses have on our country. And this trend appears throughout the world. I firmly believe that small businesses can change the world.

This book, *Trucking Business Startup*, is a way to feed you the right information and knowledge to start your own successful small business. Unlike others who start trucking businesses without setting the right foundations, you'll be different and improve your odds of success.

The journey to starting a trucking business begins with the first chapter that shows what the industry has to offer you. Go ahead and find out right away!

Chapter 1
Why a Trucking Business

To succeed in every business, including the trucking business, you need a regular flow of customers and income. This helps your business to stay afloat because it can afford to pay all its bills on time. For this to happen, it's necessary to enter a competitive industry with proven prospects of growth. Now, does the trucking industry in the United States meet these requirements? Let's dive into the industry and investigate.

Trucking companies play a vital role in moving different kinds of goods throughout the United States. Look around you for a moment. You own a refrigerator to cool and chill food and beverages so that they are tasty and stay fresh for longer. Have you ever given a thought to how it moved from the manufacturer to your home? The manufacturer had to transport it to a wholesaler, who in turn, hauled it to your local retailer. Then your local store brought it to you with a truck.

Take any other item in your home like your computer, bed, clothing, and windows and it got delivered to your home with a truck. So, truck companies play an enormous distribution role in the whole value chain from manufacturing to the consumption of goods. In 2019, trucks carried 72.5% (by weight) of all freight in the U.S. That's almost three-fourths of all the goods moved in just one year. In tonnage terms, 2019 saw this industry hauling 11.84 billion tons of goods (American Trucking Associations, n.d.).

This represents a tonnage growth of 1.04 or 9.63% from the 2017 freight weight of 10.8 tons (John, 2019). In 2017, the trucking industry moved around 70 percent of all freight in the U.S. As you can see, 2019 grew by about 2.5%. In absolute numbers, this is an incredible amount.

Furthermore, the trucking industry generated 791.7 billion U.S. dollars in 2019 (John, 2019). To put the size of this industry into perspective, its 2019 revenue is larger than the gross domestic product (GDP) of Bangladesh and many other countries. If the trucking industry were a country, it would rank 33rd going by GDP! On the employment front, the trucking industry hired around 7.4 million people. This represented 5.8% of all full-time employees in the U.S.

Imagine the industry stop working for a few days or a week! What do you think the impact would be throughout the country? Chaos. For example, stores would run out of food that citizens need to function normally. Other industries like construction, import and export would suffer greatly. In short, the country could stall. And life for most people would change completely. Experts predict that if trucks were to stop for three consecutive days, stores would run out of food. That's tragic for us as consumers, isn't it?

With a large chunk of revenue coming domestically, the trucking industry faces little exposure to direct foreign exchange fluctuations. This can give your trucking company stability, something that is crucial for planning and executing those plans.

The trucking industry often indicates the health of the U.S. economy. When the economy swings upwards, the industry's customers move more and more freight to meet consumer demand. On the other hand, a low trucking demand indicates the start of an economic downturn.

Outlook of the Trucking Industry

We have now looked at the current and past performance of the trucking industry. To complete the sustainability picture of the industry, we now look into the future. Yes, no one can predict the future, but we can have a good sense of what to expect in a few years to come with an understanding of the past.

Around mid-2018 the trucking industry reached a peak and then began an 18-month downturn. As a result, carriers saw decreased truck orders. As if that wasn't enough, insurance premiums increased. This put pressure on many trucking companies and led to increased bankruptcies.

Things began to improve soon after the downturn period and the outlook seems bright. Contract truckload volumes have increased by 27%, even during a period that normally declines (Della Rosa, 2020). You may be wondering what increased demand for trucks. You see, the government greatly stimulated our economy financially and increased the unemployment benefits. These interventions resulted in increased consumer spending. And the effect filtered through to the supply chain and positively impacted the trucking companies. As a result, truckload volumes have shot up by 25% compared to 2018 levels (Della Rosa, 2020).

This bodes well for the truck companies as industry experts expect contract rate negotiations to stay unchanged or increase in single digits. In addition, the capacity is tight and spot prices keep growing. The national load spot rates jumped 25% compared to 2019 levels (Della Rosa, 2020). With improving rates, carriers are likely to see higher profits and the timing couldn't be better to start a trucking business.

Just so you don't get confused, let me explain the difference between spot rates and contract rates. Spot rates are short-term truckload prices. Twenty percent of the trucking market comes from spot rates. In contrast, contract rates are long-term freight prices subject to either party's adjustments when they deem it necessary. This often occurs when the supply and demand equation changes. The remaining 80 percent of the freight market comes from these contract rates.

The next significant trucking business influencing factor is the ongoing truck driver shortage. Coupled with rising freight demand and increasing truckload prices, this situation paints a welcoming picture for new trucking businesses. In 2018, the trucking industry had a shortfall of about 900,000 qualified truck drivers (Raphelson, 2018). This means that the industry battled to cater to its market fully. Thus, trucking freight customers had to find other ways to get their goods delivered in time and cost-effectively to their destination.

This is an excellent opportunity for you to join the industry and help it meet customer trucking demands. Experts predict that conditions in the trucking industry will likely remain strong and gradually improve. In fact, these experts see the sector growing by 27% in the next 10 years! That's welcome news to a person like you. But there's more good news.

Small trucking companies dominate the trucking industry, with 91% of them running their businesses with six or fewer trucks (Corporation Service Company, n.d.). This indicates that you can get business in the industry even if you are a beginner. Now, if you empower yourself with the right knowledge and skills, you'll be able to reap extraordinary economic results in this industry. And you've already taken the first step in gathering the required knowledge and skills by purchasing this book.

Factors That Influence the Trucking Industry

It's essential to arm yourself with the right knowledge before starting any business. More importantly, you need to know those niggling issues that could derail your ambitions. The same applies to the trucking business. There are factors that every carrier owner should know and take into consideration in their strategic planning. Let's discuss seven of the most important factors.

1. **Supply of Truck Drivers**

    A trucking business cannot survive even a day without drivers. Truck driving is a demanding job because you can spend days away from home and far from friends. Then there are government regulations, the weather, and schedules that require a great deal of responsibility. Overall, the lifestyle of truck drivers doesn't appeal to many people. Earlier I shared that the U.S. trucking industry is in dire need of qualified drivers.

The aging of current drivers has exacerbated the situation even more. Furthermore, the industry is seeing dropping numbers of employees who choose truck driving as their profession. As a result, businesses battle to keep or find qualified truck drivers. This forces Trucking business owners to offer their drivers better salaries to keep them for longer or to attract new drivers.

This situation isn't ideal for a trucking business start up because it can lead to increased overhead and reduce its survival chances. You may wish to consider driving your own truck in the beginning if you're already qualified. If you prefer to hire drivers, your negotiation skills need to be sharp to avoid overpaying. Perhaps you might consider other benefits like stock options for your drivers instead of hiring them at large salaries.

2. **Fuel Cost**

Trucks run on diesel, a product of oil refining. For this reason, your fuel cost will be affected by the changing oil prices. The unfortunate thing is that a carrier has no control over the price of oil. High fuel prices force you to forward the cost to your customers to remain profitable. Unfortunately, you may become less price competitive and lose some customers. This may lead to running fewer trucks. And this is not good for a trucking business.

However, you can control, to a certain extent, the fuel efficiency of each truck in your fleet. Right from the beginning, you should work out the fuel efficiency that makes each truck profitable, and then control future fuel costs around that baseline figure. Of course, the way the driver operates the truck would influence fuel efficiency. Hence, having skilled drivers not only shields you from safety issues but can help keep your business running costs low as well.

3. **Market Changes**

When the U.S. economy grows, trucks' demand follows suit because more freight needs to be moved. The opposite is also true. This means that the trucking business is seasonal. For example, when the holidays approach, shipping activity generally increases in anticipation of higher consumer demand. As such, spot rates also increase, resulting in trucking businesses making more money.

4. **Weather Events**

Natural disasters, such as hurricanes and winter storms, can negatively impact the truck industry. During these times, it's challenging to drive and the number of loads delivered drops. This results in decreased revenues for affected trucking businesses. Weather delays can cost carriers somewhere between $2.2 to $3.5 billion annually. Unfortunately, as a trucking business owner you have no control over natural weather events.

5. **Changing Government Regulations**

As you'll learn in Chapters 2 and 3, a trucking company must comply with several groups of regulations, such as safety and tax. There are many government regulations and organizations that can potentially affect your carrier. Some of these government arms include the Department of Transportation (DOT), the Federal Motor Carrier Safety Administration (FMCSA), the Occupational Safety and Health Administration (OSH), the Department of Labor (DOL) and many other federal, state, and local regulatory agencies.

To keep up with all the necessary regulations costs money. And thus, changing regulations could affect your profitability.

6. **Carrier Capacity**

The factors I've discussed above can result in some trucking businesses filing for bankruptcy, especially the less established carriers. For example, when larger carriers raise driver salaries, smaller trucking companies tend to find it challenging to match their larger competitors' wages. As a result, these smaller companies lose drivers to larger carriers and face the inevitable: filing for bankruptcy.

7. **Theft or Loss**

Theft in the trucking industry occurs either internally or externally. Internal theft takes place when your own employees steal from you. On the other hand, external theft involves someone unlinked to your carrier.

Shippers prefer to hire truckers that always deliver their freight to target destinations. When your business is often a victim of theft, especially internally, your reputation suffers. And this can make it difficult for you to get business.

Another common form of internal theft is the stealing of fuel. Luckily, there are technologies to help you to prevent this loss. But if your own employees steal the goods that your business delivers, then you'll face a serious trust challenge from shippers. So, you'll need to have systems in place to prevent theft.

Those are some of the factors that could affect your trucking business. Now, I'd like to talk with you about the good and the bad of a trucking business.

The Pros of a Trucking Business

Everything created by humans has both pros and cons. So it is with a trucking business. Let's first look at the pros.

- **Independence**. When you're working for someone, you have limited decisions that you can make. Besides, you may have to pass your decisions by your boss for them to be implemented. But running your own trucking business allows you to make and implement your own decisions. One key decision that you have to make is which trucking niche to operate in. You may decide to support food manufacturers, construction companies or makers of electronics.

You're also free to choose the days of the week for work and the days when you're off. But you should know that the decisions you make and the control you have come with responsibility and accountability.

- **Flexibility**. Working for yourself provides more freedom than working for someone else. The reason is that you have the freedom to work on your own terms. You're free to run your own schedule. Furthermore, you depend far more on yourself to deliver the results that you promise your customers.

- **Profitability**. When working for another carrier, you earn a salary over which you have little control. But running your own carrier provides you with an opportunity to make more because you can generate a lot more profit. Most importantly, you can determine the level of profit per load you want because you set up the shipment contract and deliver the freight.

Let's now turn our attention to the cons of a trucking business.

The Cons of Running Your Own Carrier

Not all is rosy when running your own trucking company. Here are some challenges you'll likely face.

- **Time-consuming**. When driving for a large carrier, your main job is simply to drive and deliver the freights. An owner-operator or trucking business owner has a lot more to do. For example, you'll have to ensure that the business runs as smoothly as possible, obtain funding (if necessary), and ensure that the trucks' maintenance occurs without failure. Furthermore, you need to find customers and prepare contracts.

So, you may not have much free time, especially in the beginning. However, suppose you resolve from the start to build systems for business operations like sales and marketing, operational procedures, safety procedures, and so on. In that case, you'll soon free up a lot of time.

- **Responsibility**. Owning and running your own trucking business comes with benefits. However, the perks mean that you have to be responsible for a lot more. If the business isn't finding customers, you'll have to figure out why and solve the problem. One vital area that you will need to be on top of is ensuring that you comply with all applicable government regulations.

- **Stress.** Starting any business from scratch isn't easy, let alone a trucking company in an industry with so many regulations. It can be tough to get good customers and the right load prices. In trucking, a carrier's reputation enhances the chances of becoming a profitable business. But being a start-up that lacks the reputation of an established business can be immensely stressful.

153

Another strain-causing area is ensuring that you have the funds to run your business efficiently. So, you need to network intelligently to find the capital as well as profitable trucking loads to build your brand. Initially, you may have to learn new skills and this isn't a walk in the park.

- **High start-up costs**. Starting a trucking company can be capital-intensive because of the type of equipment you need to have. So, you may need to develop skills to find funds quickly. Luckily, there are financing options in the transportation industry to help you get started right. If you do your homework thoroughly, becoming your own boss can soon be a reality.

Now you have a good idea of the trucking industry and the potential business opportunity it offers. You also know the positives and the challenges that are common in the industry. If you're after freedom and flexibility, and can ride some short-term challenges like stress, then the trucking business is ideal for you. So, read on to find out what, specifically, you need to know about the trucking business before you start.

Chapter 2
What to Know Before You Start

Business is like war. It requires thorough preparation and strategy before getting into it. Going in blind can obliterate your business in no time. Hence, this chapter details the costs associated with starting a trucking business and how to determine the profitability of your enterprise. Most importantly, this chapter includes a plan that you can use as a roadmap so that you can begin your trucking company on the right footing and increase your chances of survival.

What to Expect When Running a Trucking Business

There is no secret that owning and running a trucking business successfully is hard work. You'll likely spend a big chunk of your time (if you are an owner-operator) hauling for your customers. Add to this the other duties small business operators have to perform, such as finding customers and building relationships, and you have a demanding task ahead of you. All these tasks require your time. This means that you may have to spend more time away from home, especially in the beginning, while putting the various business systems together.

Safety Rules and Regulations

Compliance with safety rules and regulations is essential in the trucking industry. There are plenty of these rules and regulations, which I'll talk about in more detail later in the book. Some of them include the following:

- Canadian Safety Association (CSA) safety standards (where applicable).

- The allowable hours of work for your drivers.

- Physical qualifications for truck drivers.

- Electronic logging devices for each driver to figure out the weekly hours they have worked.

Don't think of these regulations as a way to punish you. In fact, they may even dissuade others from joining the industry and thus improve your prospects of succeeding.

Costs of Starting and Owning a Trucking Company

The question of the amount of money you need to start a trucking company provides different views and answers. This is because start-up costs depend on several factors, such as the state that you're in, the size of your fleet, whether you already own a truck and have insurance, and whether you'll haul freight interstate, intrastate, or both.

Typically, a small trucking company costs about $25,000 to $40,000 to get started. This figure excludes the costs of purchasing equipment. Here are the major expenses you'll pay during the truck business start-up phase:

- Insurance down payment of between $2,000 and $4,800 a truck annually.

- The price of a truck. Which varies from $15,000 to $175,000 depending on its condition, type, and age or if you choose to buy one outright.

- State-specific tax of about $500 a truck.

- International Registration Plan (IRP) costs between $500 and $3,000.

- Business registration costs from $50 to $300, depending on your state.

- USDOT (Motor Carrier) number costs from $300 to $499.

- The International Fuel Tax Agreement (IFTA) report costs around $150.

- Unified Carrier Registration (UCR) of $69 and above.

- Trucking insurance ranging from $9,000 to $12,000 a truck annually.

- Appointing a Blanket of Coverage (BOC-3) processing agent costs from $10 to $50.

Adding up all the expenses listed above means that you'll need to set aside from $28,000 to $200,000. Note that this is an estimate. You still need to work out the exact amounts of each expense necessary to start your company. In addition, you need to factor in other expenses, such as meals, salaries, bookkeeping, parking, and tolls.

Why You Should Start With One Truck

Nothing beats growing a business organically. What do I mean by this? You see, you can choose to buy six trucks at the start of your business. If you start such a trucking business from scratch with no knowledge, skills, and experience, then the mistakes you're bound to make can wipe out the company in no time. This happens because you would have tried to jump the growth steps necessary to build the right competencies. And without the required fundamental skills, the chances of succeeding diminish greatly.

It is like these people who win the lottery and wind up broke within a few years. The lottery windfall finds them with no money management skills and all the bad habits of living. Most of them, inevitably, focus on consumption and soon use up all the money. They, essentially, return to the level where they were before winning the lottery. Money, like all tools, is an accelerator. And you can only safely accelerate something that's built on a sound foundation.

Starting with one truck provides ample opportunities to learn safely while making money. Here are some advantages of this approach:

- You reduce the amount of start-up capital to a manageable level. This minimizes the stress of looking for funding, which is better for you and your family.

- You minimize the risk of business loss. One truck means less complexity. And the simpler the business, the easier it is to run and to correct mistakes quickly. Big companies do not have the ability to respond swiftly when changes need to be made. But you will if you're operating with a single truck.

- Provides the opportunity to learn from your mistakes without putting the business at too much risk.

- Most importantly, you give yourself the time to build systems to run your business more efficiently in the future. Think about this for a moment. Would it be easier to build a safety system for one truck or for a fleet of ten? Of course, it would be easier to do so if you run one truck. And when you add a second truck, all you do is duplicate what you would have already done. This means that you'll grow your business quicker as time progresses.

The systems to consider building while operating one truck include human resources, information technology, marketing, sales, operations, technology, and so on. The power of a system is that it frees resources and enables you to do more with less. For example, with a system you can onboard a new driver much faster than another business and make fewer mistakes. Furthermore, systems allow you to deliver consistent performance, which is key to building a reputation that is so necessary in the trucking industry.

What Profits Can I Make in a Trucking Business

The profitability of your trucking business, like in any business, depends largely on how well you run your company. Well-planned trucking businesses that manage cash flow and avoid deadhead miles average around 7% of gross income per year in profit. This means that, for a company generating $300,000 of annual revenue per truck, it will profit $21,000 from every truck.

The timing of getting paid after doing the work affects your business profitability. Late payments may push you to begin shortcutting important work like truck maintenance or borrow a lot more. If you don't do maintenance in time, your trucks may often break down and cost you more in repairs. The repair costs will eat away at your profits. Borrowing money isn't free. It costs money and can pull your business back instead of strengthening it.

Furthermore, as a start-up, keep in mind that it may take several months before your company turns a sizable profit. This reason, and the one above, provide convincing evidence why having three to six months of emergency cash is so vital for your business. It will help you weather the storm in the event that you meet unforeseen events and circumstances.

You're probably wondering how much money you'll personally make when running your own trucking company. Well, this depends on your skills, experience, and competency. If you are good at getting customers and delivering what you promise, you'll make more money than the average small carrier. Trucking business owners with more experience can make around $100,000 or more, while the less experienced earn about $35,000 per year. Most owners make a healthy $50,000 annually (CDL.com, n.d.).

Do keep in mind that you'll need to provide your own truck, buy truck insurance, maintenance, and fuel. So, you do a lot more work than a driver working for a large carrier. However, your focus is not just to make money but to build an asset that will deliver cash flow even when you're no longer actively working. This can only happen if you build effective systems to run your business.

How to Estimate the Revenue of Your Trucking Company

It is important before you start your trucking company to know what revenue to expect. You're fortunate because the way to figure out your potential revenue is already available. And I'll show you here how to do it painlessly. There is no standard revenue per mile available in the industry. So, you have to figure out your own numbers. Here's how to do it.

1. **Select the Industry to Support**

    Your first task is to choose the industry in which you want to operate. This is important, as you'll see below when choosing a freight lane. More importantly, doing this enables you to buy the right truck. Imagine buying a reefer and choosing projects that require a flatbed. That would be catastrophic, isn't it?

    So, choosing the industry precedes the purchasing of equipment. For example, if you choose to serve the fresh produce industry, you'll need to buy a reefer. Furthermore, selecting the industry helps you to learn the specifics like seasonality and price variations. This, in turn, allows you to plan your business much better than without this knowledge and information.

2. **Choose Freight Lane to Work**

A freight lane, also called a carrier lane or shipping lane, is a route that you routinely run to deliver truckloads. It runs from point A to point B. For example, it could run from New York to Los Angeles.

Now, it's vital to select a shipping lane that services your chosen industry and is closer to where you live. The latter is vital because you'll be able to maximize the time you spend at home. There are truck drivers that barely see their homes for days or weeks. And this may not be optimal for building healthy family relationships.

Ensure that you select carrier lanes that are near transportation "hot markets." Why is this important? Because it is easier to find loads where the demand is high. Markets like Chicago, Atlanta, Memphis, Texas, Louisiana, Seattle, and California are busy trucking companies.

3. **Figure Out the Pay-Per-Mile on Your Carrier Lane**

The following six steps will not only show you how to determine pay-per-mile on your carrier lane, but will also reveal the profitability of your shipping lane. Let's go over the six steps.

- The first thing to do is to go to a free trucking load board and look for freight in your shipping lane. A load board is nothing but an online system that lets shippers and freight brokers broadcast their freight loads.

- Second, get prices per mile on a minimum of 10 truck loads. The more, the better because the accuracy of your figures will improve.

- Thirdly, add the prices of each of the 10 loads and their corresponding miles. Now divide the total of the prices by the total number of miles. The number you have computed is the average price of each load per mile of the lane.

  Alternatively, compute each load's pay-per-mile by dividing the price by the total number of miles of each load. Then, add all the pay-per-mile numbers and divide the final answer by 10. That gives you the average price per mile of your selected freight lane in one direction.

  Now you want to know the average price per mile of the same reverse lane. It's easy to do this. Simply repeat what you did above but in the reverse lane. You may find that the two prices differ. It's not uncommon for this to happen because of the role of supply and demand.

4. **Determine the Estimated Shipper Price**

This step is vital because at some point, you'd like to work directly with shippers instead of brokers. That way you can command higher prices per mile and make more revenue and profits. You see, freight brokers advertise their loads on freight boards without the markups (money added on top of the price of an item to make a profit). It's not uncommon for these brokers to add 15%, 20%, or more for their services onto the freight price you see on load boards. The price you see on the load board is what they pay you while they keep the markup.

When you know what shippers are willing to pay, you could quote competitively and thus obtain more profit. To find what shippers are comfortable paying per load per mile, let's consider an example.

Suppose a broker's cost on your freight lane is $2.70 per mile and their markup is 20%. To obtain the shipper price, all you do is divide $2.70 by 80% (that is, 100% minus 20%). And you obtain $3.38 per mile. This figure is what the shipper pays the broker. And the broker will pay $2.70 from this figure and keep a profit of $0.68 per mile.

Now that you know what the shippers pay, you can begin to market your business directly to shippers. Doing this quickly increases your pay per load and improves your profitability.

5. **Figure Out the Monthly Profitability of Your Shipping Lane**

One of the key reasons for going into business for yourself is to make as much profit as you can. So, let's work out how much monthly profit you could make on your carrier lane.

First, add the earnings per load to a destination to the amount in the return trip. This is the total income for one round-trip. By the way, a round-trip is the distance covered from a point to a destination and back to the same point. Now, multiply the total income by the number of round-trips you can reasonably complete in a month. The outcome is your monthly revenue.

Next, work out your total monthly expenses. This includes costs for fuel, parking, meals, tolls, maintenance, salaries, and so on. Subtract the expenses from the total monthly income to get your profit. Assess the number to determine if it's the kind of profit that you're comfortable with. If not, you may have to tweak either the revenue side or the expenses side to get the profit you want. We'll discuss managing finances later in the book.

Four Types of Trucking Businesses You Can Start and Run

The carrier industry consists of several types of businesses. The most common include for-hire truckload carriers, full truckload (FTL), less-than-truckload (LTL), and couriers. Which of these you want to run depends on your needs, skills, and knowledge. Let me take through each one of them in detail for you to make an informed decision.

1. **For-Hire Truckload Carriers**

The for-hire truckload businesses haul freight belonging to other companies for money. These businesses do not manufacture or produce anything. What they do is offer a freight loading capacity to businesses that require logistic support. In essence, they hire out trucks, trailers, semi-trailers, and drivers.

The success of these carriers depends on the shipping demands of producers and manufacturers. Such a carrier requires savvy marketing and sales skills to outbid competitors and obtain freight contracts to win business. Your business could win a shipping contract for a given period, but there's no guarantee of keeping the contract when it's due for renewal. However, the good thing is that you can hedge the loss of contracts by having multiple customers.

2. Full Truckload (FTL)

As the name suggests, full truckload carriers run fleets of trucks that carry dedicated shipments for their customers. The main advantage is that a truck reaches its destination quicker because it goes directly from the loading point to the delivery location. There are no pickups or drop-offs along the way to the destination.

Shippers like the fact that there is less handling of goods as this lowers the chances of loss or damage. Full truckloads are less restricted by size and weight.

3. Less-Than-Truckload (LTL)

Less-than-truckload companies carry multiple shipments at the same time. However, the goods are often taken to different destinations. These kinds of companies operate similarly to carpooling.

Less-than truckloads work well for smaller shipments and are often cheaper than FTL for the shippers. A customer pays according to the weight of their shipment. To optimize the available space, it's better to load one to six pallets.

Unlike FTL, LTL could result in loss or damage to goods because of multiple handling along the way. This isn't a good thing for shippers. But, as a trucker, you can ensure the shipper's goods to encourage them to do business with you.

4. **Couriers**

Couriers are door-to-door companies that often deliver goods the same day to most places. Their major competition is the standard mail delivery. The dominating benefit of couriers over standard mail delivery is that they tend to deliver quicker.

The driver personally collects and delivers the item to the receiver. Because of the personal touch involved, couriers reduce the chances of loss or damage to goods. It's possible to provide a dedicated courier truck or van to your customer to give a customized service. This helps to strengthen your business relationship with shippers.

Those are the four major trucking business options that you have and can select from. Irrespective of the trucking option you choose, you still need to decide whether you'll hire drivers or become an owner-operator. And the choice you make will dictate how you operate your business.

The final decision depends mainly on the more cost-effective approach. Most importantly, your business skills will help you decide the better route to follow. If you desire to drive a truck, perhaps becoming an owner-operator is the right route for you. However, you should know that it is hard work.

Prepare and Craft a Business Plan

Lack of planning is one of the factors responsible for business failure. Creating a business plan is a trusted way of alleviating this problem. What is a business plan? It's simply a roadmap that has a clear target that shows where you're taking your company and how you'll do it. Contrary to what some people think, a business plan doesn't have to be a 500-page document detailing every action you will take while building your business in the next 10 or 20 years.

A business plan offers a blueprint that guides you towards attaining your business goal(s). When written thoughtfully, a business plan serves several purposes. Firstly, it helps you to apply and successfully get business funding for your trucking company. This is the money that you can use to buy additional trucks if you want to expand. Secondly, a business plan shows how you're going to sell your products and services and thus generates cash flow, the lifeblood of any company.

Your business plan should include the following sections:

- **The executive summary**: This provides a short overview of your trucking company and plans to achieve your business goal(s). It's a good idea to write it last, after completing the other parts.

- **Company description**: Here you provide the business background. It's vital to include what sets your trucking company apart from its competitors. Without uniqueness, your business will just look like the rest and fail to attract your target customers' attention. Furthermore, provide details of who owns and manages the business as well as the roles and responsibilities of the employees (if applicable).

- **Services**: This section delivers an outline of the services that you'll offer to your target market. It also tells how you plan to meet customer and market demand. It's a good idea to reveal your pricing structure, the goods you plan to load and the industries you'll support.

- **Market Analysis**: This section is the heart of your business plan. It provides data that proves that there is a market for your business. It shows how you plan to win new business and beat your competitors. Some components to include here are:

  - Description of the trucking industry and its outlook.

  - Who is your target market and where you'll find them.

- Pricing and the profit margin.

- Competitor analysis. This means telling the weaknesses and strengths of your rivals to show how you discovered a competitive advantage.

- The regulatory environment and how it can impact your business. Importantly, you need to show how you'll handle regulatory challenges.

- **Sales and Marketing**: Together with market analysis, the sales and marketing sections make up a considerable chunk of your business plan's value. This section focuses on providing strategies to find prospective customers. It doesn't help much to only find customers, you still must generate cash from them. Divide this section into two subsections like this:

  - **Marketing strategy**: This subsection details exactly what you'll do to get clients and grow your base of customers. Mention the means you'll use to market your company, such as direct mail, networking, online marketing, and social media. It's vital to include an estimate of your marketing budget to meet your identified objectives.

  - **Sales Strategy**: Here you need to explain how you'll turn prospects into customers who buy. Spell out how you'll sell your services. Are you going to hire sales agents or a third party? Think through your selling strategies carefully because there's no cash flow without sales and, therefore, no business.

- **Funding request**: If you're producing the business plan for funding purposes, this is the section to spell that out clearly. You need to be clear about the amount of money you request and its purpose. Most importantly, include what you'll give in return for the funds, such as equity. Don't overlook spelling out the terms of your offer, such as the exit strategy both for you and your funder(s).

- **Financial projections**: The financial projections will depend on the trucking industry's outlook and your market share. The numbers that you include here should cover the break-even analysis. Most importantly, include in your projections your balance sheet, profit and loss statement, cash flow statement, and the sales forecast.

Those are all the key sections to include in your plan. Even if you're not going to seek funding, it helps to go through the business planning process. The reason you do this is to ensure you think through all aspects of your trucking business. That way, you'll improve your chances of survival.

Eight Must-Know Reasons Why Trucking Businesses Fail

I've just gone through the business planning process with you to avoid starting a carrier with minimal chances of survival. I did that because 85% of trucking companies fail in their first year of operations. This means that a mere 15% see the second year (CDL.com, n.d.). Isn't it essential to know why there is such a high failure rate of trucking companies? It is vital to know and I'll share with you the eight reasons why these businesses fold so quickly.

1. **Inadequate Business Planning**

   A plan tells you where you are and where you're going. Unfortunately, owners of some trucking businesses fail to craft thoughtful business plans. And as a consequence, their companies fail to survive, some not even the first year. It is for his reason why I included the previous section in this book.

   The trucking industry has many regulations plus a unique target market. You need to think through these aspects of a trucking business to understand the industry and plan how you'll reach your goals. For example, your plan should be clear about how you'll handle these regulations and future changes. Furthermore, you need to think about how you'll build relationships with your target market.

   Most importantly, it's vital to review your plan at regular intervals, such as quarterly or half-yearly, to ensure you're still on track. Or to adjust the plan, if need be.

2. **Poor Business Management**

   I've always found it difficult to manage anything that I don't measure. To manage means to ensure something does what it is supposed to do. This means that you first need to define what your business should do. And this is where your business plan comes in and provides the business measures to work towards.

When you begin running your business, it's vital to keep numbers such as sales, number of customers, miles you're covering, the freight lanes you're working, and so on. Then you'd be able to determine whether you are running your business according to the plan you would have crafted or not.

There are two major groups of numbers to keep. The financial numbers which you can record and keep yourself or for which you could hire a bookkeeper. These numbers tell you quickly where the money is coming from, how much of it there is, and where it goes. The second group of numbers comes from your operations. They are operations numbers that indicate how efficient you're running your business. Such numbers include the number of round-trips you complete per week, month, and year.

Keeping numbers is a big part of running any successful business. Without keeping a scorecard in a basketball match, how do you know who won? So it is in the trucking business. So, ensure you keep the right numbers.

3. **Inadequate Cash Flow**

When a trucking business doesn't bring in money, often owners say that they have a cash flow problem.

Yet, a careful look into the business will reveal that the problem isn't cash flow. If cash flow were the problem, solutions would focus on it. But a short time in business will reveal to you that cash flow is a result of business activities like sales and cost control.

So, inadequate cash flow is the outcome of a business operation that's gone wrong. Some of those issues include the following:

- Not getting enough customers.

- Having several outstanding invoices.

- High cost of operations such as excessive truck breakdowns and truck fuel inefficiency.

To solve these problems, you should first analyze your business numbers to locate those responsible for low cash flow. Then figure out ways to solve them one at a time. For quick cash flow improvement, I suggest solving the high-impact issue first.

4. **No or Ineffective Collection Strategy**

Your customers are unlikely to pay you cash for your trucking services. They may commit to paying you in 30, 45, or 60 days after invoicing them. Still, when the invoice is due, they may not be able to pay.

That's where your collection system kicks in. This system will help you to identify unpaid accounts well in time and act swiftly. With an effective collection strategy, you'll notice fewer cash flow issues due to unpaid invoices. I'll provide details in Chapter 6 on what to include in your collection strategy.

5. **Lack of Knowledge of Market Rates**

We covered market rates of freight lanes earlier in the book. At this point, you should be familiar with how to determine your carrier lane's pay-per-mile. This enables you to quote your customers correctly. If you're underquoting for some weird reason, nothing prevents you from adjusting your rates in future loads.

Without adjusting, your rates could land your business in negative profit territory. And no business can survive for long with no profit. This is because such a business will need a cash injection from elsewhere to close the cash flow gaps. And that's not a positive sign of a profitable business.

6. **Non-Compliance to Legal and Safety Regulations**

I'm sure by now you're noticing that most of the factors that result in trucking business failures are related to business planning. If you recall, one of the items to think through during business planning is the regulatory environment. Unfortunately, some trucking businesses overlook doing this work upfront. And soon enough, their misstep catches up with them. I don't want you to be a victim of this oversight.

Also, regulations often change. Are you geared to catch them and adjust your business when this happens? You should. This means that you need to have ways to keep track of applicable regulatory changes. Failure to catch and comply with regulations could result in fines and possible shutdown by the Department of Transportation (DOT). Furthermore, complying with regulations minimizes headaches and stress, and helps you to run your carrier profitably.

One of the powerful things to do is to write a detailed safety plan. Then, you need to keep training and refreshing your drivers so that they stay informed and competent to comply with transportation law.

7. **Forming Partnerships With the Wrong People**

Business partnerships can be great. Partners share work and contribute resources like capital. The load of running a trucking business becomes lighter. But things can go wrong. One or more of the partners may begin to abdicate their responsibility. And this could create tensions and possible business failure.

Entering into a legal partnership agreement that spells out each partner's responsibility provides some protection. It's vital to ensure that you include an exit strategy in the agreement that protects both partners. In fact, any contract or agreement that you enter into should have an exit strategy to protect you from possible financial ruin.

8. **The Owners Fail to Seek Professional Help**

A trucking business has several aspects that need to be taken care of. Some activities that need regular attention include accounting, safety management, vehicle maintenance, marketing, law, and sales. Sometimes (and it often happens), it can be hard to cover all of them because you have a limited amount of time, energy, and mental power. You don't have to let your business suffer because of this.

There are professionals, like bookkeepers, lawyers, safety managers, and so on, who can help reduce your workload. Not only will you free up some of your time and energy, but you'll also think clearer and run your business better. However, keep in mind that delegation doesn't mean you're not responsible. You still need to ensure those who help you do the right work because the buck stops with you in your business.

You're now in a position to begin learning how to get started with your trucking company.

Chapter 3
Getting Started

This chapter will take you through the steps to take to get started, from business registration to applying for business insurance. I cover all the documentation and licenses you need for you to get started right in your trucking business journey.

This information is vital because it helps you get started the right way. Let's get started right away.

Business Registration

There are four common types of business for the small business operator. You must understand each of them to select the kind that meets your needs. You have a choice of either a sole proprietorship, partnership, limited liability company, or corporation. The choice you make brings with it certain legal and financial implications. One significant implication is the taxes you'll need to pay to keep your business on a legal footing. Let's go over each of these kinds of business entities so you can make an intelligent choice.

1. **Sole Proprietorship**

   A sole proprietor is the simplest type of business entity. It's ideal for a person who owns and runs the business by themselves. By law, immediately when you start a new business as a sole owner you become a sole proprietor.

There's no need to register with the state as a sole proprietor. However, note that you might need to apply for certain licenses or permits carrying out your business. This depends on the kind of industry in which your company operates.

- **The good of a sole proprietor**
  - It is easy to file for tax when running a sole proprietor.

  - You're allowed to deduct allowable business deductions and business losses when filing your tax returns.

  - There's no need to fill in complex documentation such as meetings.

  - You don't need to register this kind of business with the state.

- **The other side of a sole proprietor**
  - You're personally liable for debts and liabilities of your business. This is the one reason why some people avoid sole proprietors when starting businesses.

  - It's tougher to access funding, such as business loans and raising money from investors.

  - Building business credit isn't easy.

2. **Limited Liability Company (LLC)**

A limited liability company protects you from personal liability in the event of lawsuits, debts, and liabilities. The reason is that your business operates separately from the business owner. It is like a separate individual with their own assets and liabilities. A potential plaintiff cannot sue you for your business liabilities. They sue your LLC directly. It requires less paperwork compared to corporations.

Your LLC can be taxed either as a sole proprietor or a corporation depending on your choice. It's possible to add more members to an LLC. However, it is slightly more pricey to create an LLC instead of a partnership or sole proprietorship. This is mainly because you must register the LLC with the state.

• **How to Set Up an LLC**

The requirements for setting up an LLC vary from one state to the next. The good thing is that the setting up process takes only from one to four hours. Here's what you need to do to register your LLC.

○ **Make a Copy of Your State's LLC Articles of Organization Form**

The Articles of Organization Form is obtainable online from your Secretary of State's website or at their offices. Find out from the Secretary's office if it's necessary to post a notice in the newspaper and their rules regarding business names.

○ **Fill Out the Articles of Organization Form**

The Articles of Organization Form is simple to fill, and you can do it by yourself. All that's required are things like the name of your business, principal office address, registered agent, and the names of members of the LLC.

○ **Post a Notice in Your Local Newspaper**

You can only post a notice in your local newspaper if it's a requirement in your state. If it's not required, then skip this step.

○ **Send Your Articles of Organization Form to Your Secretary of State**

When you have filled in your Articles of Organization form, you are ready to send it to your Secretary of State. This stage requires a filing fee that ranges from $40 to $900 and varies by state (Scott, 2018).

Some states like California charge a corporate tax that you need to pay when you set up your LLC. This fee is separate from the filing fee. So, in some states registering an LLC could be a bit expensive compared to others. Here are the costs of filing an LLC per state (Akalp, 2015):

State	Cost of filing an LLC
Alabama	$165
Alaska	$250

State	Cost of filing an LLC
Arizona	$50
Arkansas	$50
California	$75
Colorado	$50
Connecticut	$175
District of Columbia	$220
Delaware	$140
Florida	$155
Georgia	$100
Hawaii	$50
State	**Cost of filing an LLC**
Idaho	$100
Illinois	$500
Indiana	$90
Iowa	$50
Kansas	$160
Kentucky	$55
Louisiana	$100

Maine	$175
Maryland	$155
Massachusetts	$520
Michigan	$50
Minnesota	$160
Mississippi	$50
Missouri	$50
Montana	$70
Nebraska	$120
Nevada	$75
New Hampshire	$100
New Jersey	$125
New Mexico	$50
New York	$210
North Carolina	$125

State	Cost of filing an LLC
North Dakota	$135
Ohio	$125
Oklahoma	$104
Oregon	$100
Pennsylvania	$125
Rhode Island	$125
South Carolina	$110
South Dakota	$150
Tennessee	$325
Texas	$310
Utah	$72
Vermont	$125
Virginia	$104
Washington	$200
West Virginia	$132
Wisconsin	$103
Wyoming	$103

Now you know what filing fees to expect in each of the states you want to operate your trucking business.

Does Your Business Operate Under a Different Name?

Some businesses operate using names that are different from their official names. This is legal. If you plan to do this, you should file a D/B/A (Trade Name or "Fictitious" Name) with your county.

Some states require you to file your business with them. It's a good idea to check with your state to avoid trouble later on.

Licenses and Permits You Need

Your trucking business must comply with all the necessary licensing and regulations before starting to operate. Failure may result in the loss of your business and subsequent forfeiture of any money you used. There are several licenses and permits you need, including a Commercial Driver's License (CDL), operating authority, and International Fuel Tax Agreement (IFTA). Let's discuss each of these permits and licenses and how to obtain them.

A Commercial Driver's License (CDL)

A CDL is a permission to drive large, heavy trucks or vehicles carrying hazardous substances on public roads in the U.S. If you already drive for another trucking company, there's no need to read this section of the book because you already have this license.

To obtain this license, you need to nail a knowledge and skills test. Failure to pass this test may result in your CDL having unwanted restrictions. Here are the steps to follow to obtain a CDL.

- Ensure that you are 21 years or older before you apply for a CDL. If you only want to drive intrastate, you must be at least 18 years old. I advise you to check with your state for the exact age restrictions that might be in place.

- Obtain and study your state's CDL manual. This document, also called the CDL Handbook, contains the content you need to study to pass a written CDL test. You'll also find vehicle classifications and age restrictions in some states' CDL manuals. It's easy to get your copy of this manual. Head over to the internet and type in "[Your state's name] CDL manual pdf" and you'll be directed to the right place.

- Select the type of truck or vehicle and the kind of driving you want to do. CDLs cover three classes of vehicles and each of these requires specific endorsements and requirements.

- Fill and hand in your state's CDL application and pay the applicable fees. Again, the internet makes it easy to obtain this form online.

- Supply proof of identity, residency, and social security number. You may use your social security card or Medicare ID card as evidence of your social security number. As for your identity, documents like your U.S.

birth certificate and U.S. passport are acceptable. To prove residency, simply submit a recent copy of a utility bill. I suggest that you check with your state the actual acceptable documents to confirm your identity, residence, and social security number.

- Provide medical proof of fitness. To obtain a CDL, you'll be required to prove that you're medically fit to drive large commercial vehicles. You do this by supplying the Medical Examination Report Form (MCSA-5875) and the Medical Examiner's Certificate Form (MCSA-5876). Further legibility may involve checking your driving record over the previous 10 years in all states.

- Take and pay for the vision test and knowledge exam. Once you're successful with these tests, you obtain your Commercial Learner's Permit(CLP). This permit authorizes you to drive a commercial vehicle on public roads under the supervision of a qualified CDL holder.

- Obtain the CDL. After obtaining the CLP, you should wait for 14 days before you take the CDL skills test. Some states require you to complete CDL training first successfully.

There are three tests that you should pass to get your CDL, namely:

- The vehicle inspection test.

- The basic control test.

- The road test.

The easiest way to nail all the above tests is to practice each of them using the CDL manual. Because you have the CLP at this stage, I suggest that you get access to a truck and physically practice the tests on a real vehicle. Getting a coach to help you simulate the actual CDL test conditions can help you eliminate nervousness when taking the exams.

On successfully completing your CDL tests submit the filled documents for processing. You could obtain your CDL the same day or it may be delivered to you through the mail.

USDOT Number

To reiterate, a USDOT Number uniquely identifies your carrier during events like crash investigations and audits. Transporting freight in interstate commerce requires a company to register with the FMCSA and carry a USDOT Number. The USDOT Number is also required for the hauling of intrastate hazardous materials that require a safety permit. Some states require a trucking company to have a DOT Number.

One of the easiest ways to determine if you need to have a USDOT number is using an FMCSA **tool**. It will take you through a series of few questions. Once you have answered all the questions, you'll know whether you need this vital permit or not. If you find that you do need the USDOT Number, then it's time to apply for one. The FMCSA requires all new USDOT Number applicants to use the online Unified Registration System (URS) to obtain the permit. This mode of application debuted on December 12, 2015 and simplified registrations for various permits.

It takes about four to six weeks to get your USDOT Number. Upon obtaining this permit, display it on both sides of your trucks. Doors often provide an ideal location to stick the USDOT Number. Importantly, a person must be able to clearly see and read the USDOT Number from up to 50 feet away.

The USDOT Number opens the way for you to apply for the trucking authority explained below.

Trucking (Operating) Authority

A trucking authority provides evidence that the government gave your company permission to receive payment for moving freight. Instead of calling it the trucking authority, some people refer to it as the Motor Carrier (MC) number. You obtain the permit from the Federal Motor Carrier Safety Administration (FMCSA).

There are multiple authorities depending on the kind of work that you do in the freight industry. You may need to obtain the motor carrier authority, broker authority, freight forwarder authority, or both. Only apply for the authority relevant to the jobs you perform to save yourself time and money. Whatever authority you have determines the required financial responsibility to keep, such as the level of insurance you.

Unified Carrier Registration (UCR)

The Unified Carrier Registration (UCR) Plan and Agreement authorizes states to collect fees from qualifying trucking companies and brokers. These fees serve for tasks like USDOT officer training and to support state safety programs. However, not all states participate in the UCR Plan and Agreement. So, if you're only hauling goods intrastate, check with the state if they require UCR registration or not. A UCR offers officers a way to check and verify if you have active insurance coverage in states where you do business.

The application fee for UCR depends on the fleet size that qualifies to be included. Some companies may operate a fleet interstate, including in states not part of the UCR Plan and Agreement. In that case, not all the fleet may qualify for UCR registration. Registration opens on October 1 and runs through to December 31. Failure to pay UCR fees could result in fines and penalties. And so, you may wind up affecting the cash flow and profitability of your business by failing to abide by this regulation.

To apply for the UCR, simply head over to their website. You'll be asked to enter your USDOT Number and MC Number to proceed.

Heavy Vehicle Use Tax (HVUT)

The Heavy Vehicle Use Tax (HVUT) is an annual fee charged on heavy vehicles that run on public highways and weigh 55,000 pounds or more. The gross weight quoted includes the following:

- The weight of an unloaded vehicle ready to do its work.

- The weight of an unloaded trailer or semi trailer ready for service and its often used.

- The weight of the maximum freight carried by the vehicle and trailer or semitrailer combination.

The above weight determines the fees you'll to pay in the following manner (DOT Federal Highway Administration, 2020):

- For gross weight lying between 55,000 and 75,000 pounds, the fee is $100 plus $22 for every 1,000 pounds above the 55,000 pounds.

- If your vehicle weighs over 75,000, the HVUT is $550.

The HVUT is payable using Form 2290 available from the Internal Revenue Service (IRS). You don't have to file this form separately. The easiest way is to file it at the same time with your tax returns.

International Fuel Tax Agreement (IFTA)

The International Fuel Tax Agreement (IFTA) license permits you to pay fuel taxes to multiple member jurisdictions at a go. This means that you don't have to file the tax for each state separately. So, the process simplifies fuel tax payments for interstate and commercial trucking companies. Therefore, it's prudent to register your trucking company if you run interstate freight.

Not every truck qualifies to be included for IFTA purposes. The vehicle must be registered if it meets either of the following criteria (Boyers, 2020):

- The vehicle must have two axles and a gross weight of 26,000 and above.

- Any weight and has three axles or more.

- A vehicle used in combination and weighs over 26,000 pounds.

It is easy to apply for an IFTA license. Head over to your state's website and apply there. Note that the application forms may differ from one state to the next. On being successful with your application, you'll receive IFTA decals that expire on December 31 annually. The regulation gives you until March 1 of the subsequent year before you must carry new decals.

Standard Carrier Alpha Code (SCAC)

The Standard Carrier Alpha Code (SCAC) is a two- to four-letter code used to identify transportation companies. It helps the government to regulate transport services for tasks like border control and sticking to environmental standards. Most importantly, a trucking company doing business with many shippers must have it.

It's easy to get this code. All you do is head over to the National Motor Freight Traffic Association's website and apply or renew your SCAC code. The application fee to obtain the SCAC is $70 (STANDARD CARRIER ALPHA CODE (SCAC) APPLICATION, n.d.).

Blanket of Coverage (BOC-3) Permit

The blanket of coverage (BOC-3) permit authorizes the legal presence of trucking companies, freight brokers, and freight forwarders. Filling the BOC-3 Form is a way to designate process agents who represent your freight company in each state where you haul goods.

For example, if there is a legal issue against your trucking business, the process agent will accept court papers on your behalf. You're not allowed to fill the BOC-3 form by yourself. This is a task only process agents do. Your role in this is to select the process agent to complete the form for you.

It costs between $20 and $40 to get the form filled out and processed. For ease of administration, it's way better to choose a process agent who operates in all the states where you do business.

Often, business people desiring to enter the trucking industry find the processes lengthy and cumbersome. There's a way around this obstacle. Companies such as GLAuthority can help you apply for all the necessary permits for a modest fee. I advise new truck owners to understand still what's involved even if they hire such a company. If something goes wrong, you'll understand and solve it much faster than someone who doesn't.

Comply with Local Laws and Apply for Applicable laws

Rules and laws vary from state to state. Some rules are common such as the requirement to apply for a health permit if handling food products.

Register for Different Taxes

Each trucking should register for several taxes, including income tax, sales tax, and self-employment tax. You must register for all applicable taxes to keep your business away from troubles. You may have to pay taxes at federal, state, and local levels. The amount of tax you pay depends on the kinds of business activities your company does.

Let's go over the process of registering for these taxes.

1. **Obtain Employer Identification Number (EIN)**

   The Employer Identification Number is also called Federal Tax Identification Number. It is a unique nine-digit number used to identify a business for tax reasons. Having the EIN enables you to get things like business accounts and licenses. You can apply for the EIN online. The IRS asks you a series of simple questions and you provide the answers. This is the easiest and fastest way of getting the EIN.

   You need to have the following when applying for the EIN: The name and Taxpayer Identification Number of the business owner, principal officer, or general partner. This person must be the one who manages or directs the assets of the business. A business entity cannot be used for this purpose.

2. **Register for State Tax**

   Any company that does business in a state has what's called tax presence. This means that the business must pay state income, sales excise, and state employment taxes provided it has employees.

   The first step of the process is to register with the state's revenue department for income tax. However, some states like Washington, South Dakota, and

Florida don't have an income tax. So, make sure your base state requires you to pay income tax.

A business that sells products and services that attract sales tax must apply for a tax seller's permit in the state they operate. The sales tax is also called a trust fund tax. This permit allows you to collect, report, and pay the sales tax to the state. Most states have an online presence for easy registration. Not all states charge sales tax, such as Alaska, Delaware, and Montana.

If you have a tax presence in a state and hire employees, you need to register with your state's employment bureau by law. This allows you to collect income taxes from employees on behalf of the state. Furthermore, you should pay state unemployment taxes and the worker's compensation fund.

Important: If you do business in multiple states, you must register with each state for tax purposes. In the state you first register with your business is deemed a domestic entity. And in the remainder of the states you register as a foreign business entity.

3. **Income Tax**

All businesses must pay income tax based on the amount of profit they make. The form of the business dictates how you'll pay this tax. For example, a sole proprietor requires that you add net income from Schedule C and your income from other sources to determine your total tax. On the other hand, LLC owners can choose to pay tax like a sole proprietor or as a corporation. And thus, an LLC owner paying tax as a sole proprietor will pay a different tax amount than in a corporation having equal revenues.

As a business owner, the law allows you to deduct certain expenses before reporting your taxable income. The regular business expenses to deduct are numerous. The key is to ensure that you deduct only costs you incurred for business purposes. Most importantly, you must have proof for each deduction that you make. Some expenses you may deduct include the following.:

- Business meals.
- Business insurance.
- Work-related travel costs.
- Advertising and promotion.
- Professional services like accounting and office cleaning.

There's also another kind of business deduction that you can make. It is called qualified business income deduction (QBI). This law came in force in the 2018 tax year and will continue until 2025. Using QBI, you're allowed to deduct up to 20 percent of qualified business income (Murray, 2020). However, the deduction applies only for business owners who pay their business taxes on their personal tax returns.

Notice that (QBI) deduction adds to the usual acceptable business expense deductions.

4. **Self-Employment Taxes**

Self-employment taxes serve to fund Social Security and Medicare. The amount you pay depends, like income tax, on the net income of the business. This means that when your business makes no profit, there won't be a self-employment tax. It doesn't stop there. Not paying self-employment taxes results in no Social Security and Medicare credits for that year. So, if you want to increase Social Security and Medicare credits every year, you must keep making profits annually.

Not every business owner pays self-employment taxes: only sole proprietors, partners making up a partnership, and LLC owners.

5. **Sales Tax**

Sales tax gets paid on sales of qualifying products and services that businesses sell. The government charges a certain percentage on every sale of certain products and services. The good thing for the business owner is that this tax isn't your responsibility. It is the consumers who pay it.

The business's role is to collect this tax, report, and pay it to the government. You need to have a system to collect and account for sales tax to avoid mistaking it for your business revenue or profit.

6. **Gross Receipts Tax**

Most states require businesses to pay a state income tax, as we've discussed above. However, states like

197

Nevada and Texas charge gross receipts (revenue) tax, either adding to state income tax or replacing it.

Not all business types are eligible for gross receipts tax. It's therefore essential to check with your state if your business is eligible for this tax. Sole proprietors often ineligible for paying gross receipts tax although they still pay state income tax.

7. **IFTA Fuel Tax Returns**

We've already discussed what IFTA fuel taxes are. Now it's time to understand how a trucking business pays for them. The crucial thing is to ensure that you have your accurate IFTA reporting documents and file the return in time to avoid fines, penalties, and energy-sapping external audits.

IFTA fuel taxes get paid quarterly. The due dates are as follows:

- April 30 for the first quarter.
- July 31 for the second quarter.
- October 31 for the third quarter.
- January 31 of the following year for the fourth quarter.

It is easy to pay for IFTA taxes. The IFTA members have streamlined the process to allow you to pay these taxes online through the Department of Revenue's IFTA Fuel Tax System. This system can help you do more than only pay taxes.

You can use it to request additional IFTA decals and

manage other issues related to this regulation.

Preparing and paying IFTA fuel tax can be a life-sucking exercise. The way around this issue is to utilize IFTA reporting software. That way, you'll simplify the IFTA tax paying and reporting processes, save time, and improve efficiency. I show how to work out your IFTA fuel taxes in Chapter 6 so that you know how the software generates these taxes.

Receiving Payments from Your Customers

When you complete loads for your customers you want to get paid. So, you'll issue an invoice, and the customer will pay it within the agreed time. However, the customer will want to know the ways available to pay your invoice. There are several ways of receiving money for the services and products you offer to your customers. It's easier for your customers if you give them a variety of options. Whatever options you choose, you should ensure that they'll simplify your downstream processes like cost reviews and filing tax returns.

The key step before identifying any invoice payment options is to open a business bank account. There are good reasons for doing this.

Why You Should Open a Bank Account and Business Credit Card

Some business owners make a serious money management mistake. They combine their personal money with the business cash. This makes accounting for business income difficult. And that can make paying the relevant taxes a nightmare. So, to simplify your personal and business money management processes, it's essential to open separate bank accounts. One account for your business and another for personal use.

Usually, at this point, you already have a personal bank account. All you need to do now is to open a business bank account. It starts with shopping around for banks that offer cost-effective bank accounts. Also, consider the reputation of the bank when deciding where to open a bank account. One of the great benefits of a bank account is that it will simplify cost management and tax filing.

The other important money management tool is a business credit card. It helps you to keep your business expenses in one place for easy managing and control of credit. Furthermore, it helps your trucking business build a credit history, which can be handy when looking for funding to expand your fleet, for example.

Like with a bank account, shop around for a bank or credit union that offers good credit cards and rewards.

Now, let's talk about the right ways you may receive payments.

1. **Your Business Bank Account**

   Getting paid directly into your business account is the easiest method you can use. Because it's direct, the only costs you may pay will be bank charges. You don't have to do anything special to get paid this way. Simply include your business bank details in your invoice. If you prefer this method, let your customer know on the invoice.

2. **Point of Sale Payment**

Three things are necessary for you to be paid through a point of sale system. You need to have a bank account, a credit card merchant account, and a payment processing device.

It costs $50 to $200 in start-up fees and monthly transaction fees. It's not uncommon for transaction fees to be around five to 50 cents per purchase. Monthly fees often hover around $4 to $20 a month.

3. **Online Payment Systems**

Online systems have become increasingly important, especially for businesses operating online. One big player in online payment systems is PayPal. It's easy to use PayPal because you don't need to be an expert on computers. All you need is to register a business account online. Then, they'll inform you what documentation they need, if necessary.

Once your account activates, you simply locate and choose a "Buy Now" code and paste it into your website. Your customers then click on the button to pay for your services and products. They'll be taken through a simple process until the transaction completes. Transaction fees start from 0.7% to 2.9% of the invoice value plus 30 cents per order. Your sales volume will influence the actual fees that you pay.

Business Insurance

The purpose of business insurance is to protect your business and its assets financially. The kinds of insurance you need depend on the nature of your business and circumstances. What's common on all insurance is that you should shop around for cost-effective insurance products with attractive terms.

Let's talk about the types of insurances you need as a trucking business.

1. **General Liability Insurance**

   General liability insurance protects your business against financial loss due to events like bodily harm, property damage, medical expenses, defending lawsuits, and judgments. These events are often out of your control and that's where a general liability insurance comes in.

   In the freight industry, you'll need anywhere from $300,000 to $5,000,000, depending on the kinds of goods you transport (Federal Motor Carrier Safety Administration, 2019). A $1,000,000 cover finds acceptance with many shippers and freight brokers (Getloaded, n.d.).

2. **Commercial Property Insurance**

   Commercial property insurance covers loss against damage to business property, such as vehicles and buildings. Property damage may occur due to events like fire, hurricanes, and other disasters beyond your control. The value of commercial property insurance you need depends on the type and condition of the assets you protect.

3. Home-Based Business Owner's Insurance

A home-based business owner's insurance is limited liability protection covering a small amount of equipment and third party injury. It adds to your normal homeowner's insurance.

Check with your homeowner's insurer if they accept running a business at your home. Operating a business from home may attract higher premiums and deductibles.

4. Business Owner Insurance

A business owner insurance serves to simplify insurance for business owners. What it does is to bundle different insurance products into a single policy. This simplifies your business life because you only have to deal with one company and one policy instead of five or six policies.

5. Cargo Insurance

A cargo insurance protects your business against loss due to damage or loss of freight. A cargo insurance of $100,000 provides sufficient cover for most freight companies (Getloaded, n.d.). However, the exact amount of coverage depends on the type of cargo you load.

6. **Physical Damage Insurance**

A physical damage insurance protects your trucking business in case your truck gets involved in an accident where someone else is at fault.

7. **Non-Trucking Use (Bobtail) Insurance**

Non-trucking use insurance protects your business if your truck gets involved in an accident without your customer's load.

The above are the major types of insurances that you need to have in your trucking business. Where possible, try to bundle them together to minimize the amount of paperwork you need to handle. Doing so will further save you time and money.

When shopping around for insurances, ensure you do the following, amongst other things:

- Compare premiums and terms.

- Check if there's any business revenue cap for each insurance to ensure your company stays covered even when it grows.

- Ensure that you buy adequate coverage to avoid out-of-pocket expenses.

- Verify that your property and the area of business qualify for each business insurance cover.

Having registered your business and getting the required permits and licenses, you now are ready to begin building your fleet of trucks.

Chapter 4
Building Your Fleet

Starting a trucking business may seem costly and it is if you don't have the finances. Just to start, it may require in the vicinity of $20,000 to $40,000 without adding trucks. Considering that a truck can cost anywhere from $15,000 to $175,000 you're looking at a significant amount of money to start. And for a down payment, it's not uncommon to have to pay $1,000 to $10,000 depending on your vehicle choice and condition of the truck.

Despite this seemingly large amount of start-up money, you can still launch a trucking company. You don't necessarily need to have a lot of money to get started in the trucking industry. You need the right information, and this chapter shows you some funding options you have available. Before we talk about funding itself, let's discuss the kinds of trucks and costs you can expect.

Which is Better, a New or Used Truck?

Trucks are the foundation of any trucking business. Therefore, you need to have trucks that are in good condition to complete the delivery of your customers' loads. With this idea in mind, it should be easy to notice that it's not about whether the truck is new or old, but that it can do the job at hand.

However, there are advantages to buying new trucks as opposed to second-hand models. The most significant benefit of new trucks is lower maintenance. Because they're new, they'll likely give you significant mileage before beginning to have problems. But new trucks cost a lot more to purchase than second-hand types. You'll need to have at least $100,000 to buy a new truck.

On the other hand, second-hand trucks can be cost-effective, provided that their maintenance is up to date and their files are in order. Roadworthy, used trucks attract lower annual insurances, resulting in lower fixed costs for your business. This could slightly increase your profit. One example is buying a five-year-old or younger rig driven by a Detroit Diesel engine with less than 600,000 miles in it. It can still give you good, solid performance of eight to ten years but can be a bit pricey.

Although naturally you may want to save on equipment, the decision may backfire down the road. For example, you may face countless breakdowns and frequent repairs later on. This can result in higher maintenance and repair costs reducing your profits.

If you decide to buy a second-hand truck, you need to do your homework. The most important things to check for include:

- The truck's record of maintenance and history of oil changes. You want a vehicle with proof that it received maintenance in time and the right work completed each time. If you don't know how to read the maintenance record, consider finding someone competent to help you. This matter is not to be taken lightly at all.

- The condition of the tire tread.

- The mileage of the truck. The lower the mileage, the better the truck is likely to be.

- Rust on the truck's body and any other visible signs of body damage, a sign that the truck may have been involved in an accident. Such a truck is a no-go because there may be unnoticeable damage to the structure and even the truck's engine. Buying it could simply be a costly decision indeed.

There are still other important things to consider when you buy trucks.

Buy Trucks that Matches Your Business Plan

You'll recall that we spent time earlier on developing a sound business plan. This plan provided you with a chance to think about the type of customers you want to support. That immediately informs you of the type of trucks you'll need to have in your fleet. For example, to haul perishable goods, you'll need trucks equipped with refrigerated compartments to keep the items fresh.

Another factor to keep in mind is whether you'll be doing short-haul or long-haul routes. Long-haul trucks quickly rack up mileage and tend to break down more often than short-haul. So, if borrowing money, you may have to pay a more considerable amount of down payment and higher interest rates because of more risk.

Furthermore, the kind of trucks that you need for short-haul tend to differ from the long-haul vehicles. And these differences affect their prices, maintenance, and insurance.

At last, what matters is to ensure that the trucks you buy match your business plan. The reason is that you'll be able to complete your customer loads and be paid according to your expectations. And thus, you'll improve your chances of success in this tough trucking industry.

Best Makes (Brands) of Trucks

Deciding the make and model of the trucks in your fleet isn't an easy task. It doesn't matter whether you're an experienced truck driver wanting to buy a truck or you're unfamiliar with the trucking industry. It's still difficult to decide on the best make to purchase for two reasons. First, your money is involved and you don't want to make a mistake. And secondly, buying a truck is a matter of personal taste and the kinds of loads you plan to carry.

Therefore, you should take time and do thorough research, especially if you're new to the freight industry. Here are some questions to answer when choosing a brand:

- Will you be doing short-haul, long-haul, or local deliveries?

- What style of truck cab do you prefer?

- Are you buying a new or second-hand truck?

- Will you be financing, leasing, or paying in cash up front?

- Are there emission standards that the truck must meet?

Short-haul and local freight trucks don't have to have similar features as long-haul trucks. The main attribute you want in a short-haul or local truck is mechanical soundness and solid build quality. The source of the truck isn't an overly important matter. But you want to buy from a dealership that understands your business and is reputable.

On the other hand, long-haul trucks can experience breakdowns in all sorts of places. So, you want to buy the truck from a dealership with locations throughout the U.S. This ensures that you can get up and running in no time and still operate a profitable business. Brands such as Kenworth and Peterbilt have locations at strategic places throughout the country to support long-haul trucking companies.

Now, let's talk about what kind of trailers you may need for your business.

Different Types of Trailers

There are a variety of trailers that are suitable for different kinds of loading requirements. It is vital to select a trailer that will do the job efficiently.

1. **Dry Van**

    A dry van is a semitrailer with a long enclosed rectangular box sitting on wheels. It protects the freight from the weather and other things that could affect the quality of the load.

    A dry van requires a raised dock for easy loading and unloading of cargo. Some dry vans are equipped with a lift gate that enables them to load and unload freight at ground level. These trailers are common in the less-than-truckload carrying of cargo.

2. **Reefer**

A reefer is a square trailer. It has the same shape and capacity as a dry van. The difference is that a reefer boasts a refrigeration unit to maintain the temperature at certain levels. This is ideal for hauling food products that must be kept fresh by either freezing or heating.

So, a reefer must meet strict airflow regulations to maintain a set internal temperature irrespective of external weather changes. The refrigeration unit obtains power from a combination of truck power, batteries, and diesel. Because of the refrigeration unit and extra fuel, reefers take lighter loads than dry vans.

3. **Flatbed**

A flatbed is the second most common type of trailer in the U.S. trucking industry. It is the workhorse of the freight industry. Their design allows cargo to be loaded at the rear and via two lateral sides. Once loaded, bindings such as straps and chains fasten the cargo in place to prevent it from falling and getting damaged.

A closer look at the flatbed design reveals that it isn't flat throughout the deck. It bows along the length to support the freight weight without breaking. The flatbed fits transporting shipments to multiple destinations. The cargo headed the furthest could be loaded in the middle and the load that's going the nearest in the periphery. This helps to avoid damaging the shipments when loading and unloading.

4. **Step Deck**

The step deck is a variation of the flatbed. Its design allows it to easily carry taller loads. It consists of an upper-deck and a lower-deck. The upper deck's height is the same as the flatbed, while the lower-deck sits a foot and half lower. The lower deck occupies three-fourths of the trailer.

Should You Buy or Lease Trucks?

As a trucking start up business you have two options to own trucks. The first way is through the outright purchase of the vehicles. And the second approach uses the leasing method. Each of these has its pros and cons, and depends on your needs, circumstances, and financial muscles. For example, technology is advancing at a rapid rate in the trucking industry. Unfortunately, it's challenging to keep up with training and producing enough qualified technicians. As a result, you could own high tech trucks and struggle with maintenance.

Some trucking businesses choose to lease trucks, while others prefer to combine outright ownership with leasing. The decision depends on several factors, such as the type of freight you load, carrier lanes, seasonality, and type of trucks. So, it's helpful to understand how the two options differ so that you can make an informed decision.

Leasing Trucks

Leasing a truck means that you agree with a leasing company that it will provide the vehicle under the agreed terms. Then you pay a certain amount regularly (usually monthly). The amounts you usually pay do not cover the truck's full cost by the time the lease expires. At this time, you'll have various options as to how to proceed. We'll discuss this further below.

Leasing allows trucking companies to access equipment with no upfront costs and is helpful for owners with credit limitations. Often, you don't need to make any down payments. This is good because you can use the down payment elsewhere in the business, such as in marketing and promotion.

Today's trucks become obsolete quicker because of technological improvements. Leasing overcomes this challenge because it has shorter trade cycles and you can quickly upgrade to a fleet equipped with new technology.

Rental terms built into lease contracts can provide for increased capacity for seasonal work. When demand wanes, you can wind down capacity. Here's a list of top benefits of leasing:

- Trucking companies don't have to account for trucks in the balance sheet for certain kinds of leases.

- Gets rid of hidden costs involved in outright ownership of trucks.

- It frees you up to focus on key trucking business activities instead of things like maintenance

- High truck running times because of regular preventative maintenance.

Types of Leases

Leases come in varying types to cater for different trucking business needs. It's important to know which one resonates with you to become as profitable as you want.

1. **Operating (Full-Service) Lease**

   In an operating lease, the leasing business maintains the trucks and also keeps its ownership. This frees the trucking company to focus on other operational measures like driver performance and customer satisfaction.

   There are various financing options with full-service leases. You can choose the term of the lease, financing arrangements, the type of truck, and your preferred level of maintenance. However, the operating lease doesn't suit all trucking businesses.

   It's vital to do a cost analysis and let numbers tell you whether this kind of lease is the right one or not. In other words, don't go by your gut or emotions to decide if this lease suits you or not.

   If you need specialized trucks and operate where you don't need priority service, then a full-service lease might not be a good option for your business.

2. **Terminal Rental Adjustment Clause (TRAC) Lease**

A terminal rental adjustment clause lease provides for altering payment terms and lengths and offering residuals while the contract is still in force.

A truck lease takes a portion of the vehicle's cost and distributes it to be paid monthly on equal installments. The payments include interest. At the end of the lease, the vehicle has an outstanding balance not covered by your monthly payments. This remaining balance of the vehicle cost is called a residual. The leasing company retains the vehicle ownership until the lease expires.

TRAC provides an opportunity to negotiate monthly payments and the residual. So, you can opt for a higher residual with lower monthly payments or vice versa. The actual monthly payments will depend on the truck cost and how you negotiate with the leasing company. Here's what the flexible term of this lease means to you.

You may end the lease after its minimum term lapses. At this point, the leasing company either purchases or sells the truck. The money from the sale pays the balance on the original cost of the truck. It's possible to receive a refund if the selling price fully covers the residual. Or you may owe the leasing company if the selling price is lower than the truck cost.

You also may choose to purchase the truck at the agreed-upon residual when the lease expires. But you do have a choice of whether to extend the lease or not.

That's how a basic TRAC lease works. There are three more varieties of the TRAC lease.

- **Split TRAC lease**: This lease is identical to the basic TRAC lease with one major difference. The split TRAC lease protects you against market volatility. If you have a shortfall at the sale of your truck, the most you'll pay doesn't go beyond a given maximum.

- **Zero TRAC lease**: Here, the leasing company adjusts the amortization schedule to leave a zero residual at the end of the lease. This means that you become the truck owner when the lease lapses, provided that you don't take the early termination option. This suits a trucking business owner who wants to own the truck after the lease.

- **Modified TRAC lease**: Recent accounting standards require TRAC leases to be classified as capital leases for tax purposes. This means that a truck appears on your business's balance sheet as an asset. In other words, the truck appears as if it is your own. A modified TRAC lease turns this situation around and turns the TRAC lease into an operating lease. This means the truck now becomes a business expense for tax purposes. Therefore, you need to choose a TRAC lease that gives you tax advantages. And you can determine this by considering how the numbers look on either lease type.

3. **Lease-Purchase Plans**

A lease-purchase plan is a kind of lease suitable for prospective truck owners who want to own their trucks without making a down payment. It's suitable for trucking business owners who don't have a sparkling credit history.

When you enroll in a lease-purchase program, you're classified as an owner-operator right away. Owners of the lease-purchase program may supply you with a steady supply of work for you to make lease payments.

It's essential to shop around for reputable and trustworthy lease-purchase programs because they offer different benefits. Where possible, enroll in a program like this:

- Doesn't charge hidden fees. In other words, the company running the program must be transparent about all the fees that you'll be charged. Also, read the contract fully to ensure you understand what you get yourself into.

- Offers discounts on things like fuel and shopping rates.

- Is less costly. This is important because it can cost $750 to $800 a week for older trucks or

$1,100 to $1,200 to lease new vehicles. So, the lower the rates you find, the better your profits will be.

That's not all. There are lease-purchase programs that do not charge fees for Qualcomm, trailers, and cargo insurance. These businesses could result in lower expenses for your company and an improved profit position.

Let's now turn our attention to purchasing your own trucks.

Buying Your Own Trucks

Purchasing your own trucks gives you advantages that leasing does not. One great advantage is that it allows you to make significant tax deductions. It's no wonder two-thirds of trucking companies own their fleet as opposed to leasing. Perhaps some begin by leasing but do so with the intention of buying when the leases expire.

However, owning trucks brings with it several hidden costs. These are costs that you may not easily spot. They are:

- Running a maintenance workshop.

- Hiring maintenance technicians to maintain the fleet.

- Paying taxes and licensing.

- Purchasing truck consumables.

- Performing regular maintenance and attending to breakdowns.

With this in mind, it should be clear to you that, whether or not you choose to lease should be based on sound financial analysis. Business is a rational sport. If you run it primarily through emotions, you'll wind up making many mistakes. And then spend most of your time correcting these setbacks instead of moving the business forward.

When you buy trucks, they appear on your balance sheet as assets. And the loan you take becomes a liability on the same balance sheet. When you do your financial analysis to determine if leasing or purchasing is better, consider the following buying advantages:

- Buying allows you to depreciate the truck.

- Purchasing the truck affords you the luxury to deduct any interest you pay on the loan to buy the truck.

- You're permitted to deduct part or all of the money you used to buy the truck immediately. What does this mean, you may ask? Well, to answer you, let me use an example. Let's say you buy a truck for $50,000 and its salvage value at the end of five years is $7,500. By the way, salvage value is the market value of your truck at a given point in its life. As the business owner, you're allowed to deduct $42,500 ($50,000 minus $7,500) the same year of the purchase of the truck. This is like getting paid to own the truck. And you can see why you should do a financial analysis before you decide to buy or not. Ensure that you use the current IRS Section 179 for the appropriate tax deduction.

Let's say after this matter of purchasing your own truck, you decide to buy. What financing options do you have to buy the truck(s)?

How to Finance the Purchase of Your Truck(s)

Most truck companies rely heavily on financing to buy their fleet. It's understandable because purchasing a truck requires a substantial amount of money. And most don't necessarily have the cash in hand or because financing makes financial sense. Unfortunately, like banks, traditional lending institutions often don't finance trucking companies, especially if they are still new. This means that you'll have to look for financing elsewhere.

Before you head out to look for financing, pay attention to the following:

- **Get it straight in your mind what exactly you want the funding for**. Do you want to purchase one truck or more? How much would it cost? How much financing do you want? The answers to these questions lie within the pages of your business plan. This document will play a major role in securing financing, as you'll see in a moment.

- **Know that borrowing costs money**. You may be charged an interest rate of about 5% if you have a clean credit record and a sound equipment plan. On the other hand, it's common to be charged 7% to 30% when your credit record isn't as clean.

One of the financing options that you have is commercial truck funding. The advantage of this sort of financing is that it is tailored to commercial trucking. So, you deal with funders who understand your needs.

Commercial Truck Financing

Like any funding, commercial truck financing has certain requirements that you must meet before you can get the funds. Let's go over each one of them.

1. **Personal Credit History**

   Your personal credit history plays a role in your successful application for commercial truck funding. It gives funders an idea of whether you're on top of your finances or not. In other words, it tells the funders how risky you are as the business owner. A high credit score means you're less risky. Thus, you may get lower interest rates and your chances of getting funding improves.

   In contrast, a bad credit record signals that you're a higher risk when it comes to funding. And you may qualify for a higher interest rate. Or you may even not qualify for the funding.

   Don't let your personal credit score alone block you from seeking funding. Why? Because there are other factors that financiers consider that may be favorable to you.

2. **Recent Personal and Business Credit Events**

   As I said above, lenders often look at your personal credit history when applying for commercial trucking finance. They also do the same with your business credit record (if already available). Certain events can make your funding application a nightmare. Some of these include the following:

- Tax liens.

- Record of a high frequency of late payments.

- Bankruptcies.

Before you go out to look for the funds, obtain your latest credit record to check for incorrect information. If you find any, take steps to have it corrected by the credit agencies.

3. **Down Payment**

It's unlikely for commercial truck financing to cover 100% of the purchase price of the truck. Therefore, you may need to table a certain amount of down payment. The amount of down payment you have helps funders determine your seriousness, how much of a credit risk you are, and how risky a loan to you would be. The higher the down payment, the lower the risk to them and you're likely to get funding. Down payments often run from 5% to 30%.

4. **Cash in the Bank**

The amount of money in your business bank is an indication of your money habits. If you have a substantial amount of cash in the bank, you're seen as responsible. Furthermore, the lenders will likely feel that you have the skills to manage risk and have more confidence in you. They would feel that you have the ability to make the required monthly repayments. And thus, you minimize the chance of them losing money.

5. Relevant Business Documentation

Commercial truck financing lenders, like any lender, want to loan out money to legitimate entities. And the way to demonstrate that your business is legitimate is through supplying the following documents:

- Tax returns (if applicable).

- Licenses and permits.

- Financial statements, such as the balance sheet, cash flow statement, and the profit and loss statement.

- Copies of customer contracts and purchase orders (if any). Nothing proves that your business is sound than having customers.

- Bank statements.

- USDOT Number and MC number.

6. Business Track Record

The longer your trucking business's track record, the higher the chance of receiving funding. But it must be a track record that tells a good story about your business. At this point, you should be having a strong client base and a record that you deliver on your promises.

However, for a start-up, the business track record usually won't be something to write home about. So, your best bet is your business plan and any freight contracts that you may have garnered since beginning to operate. It's clear that as soon as you begin preparing to start your trucking business, you should be actively looking for customers at the same time. If you find contracts before being ready to deliver, you can hire another carrier to fulfill them for you for a fee.

7. **Type of Truck(s) You Want to Buy**

The type of truck presents its own risk to a lender. Used trucks cost less but are riskier to businesses than new ones. Furthermore, the truck's condition is vital because it should last at least until you have fully paid off the loan. Something else that's important is whether the truck will be doing short-haul or long-haul. The latter is riskier.

Vital truck information that you need to gather includes the following:

- Make and model of the truck.
- Mileage of the truck.
- Is it new or second hand?
- Complete condition report.
- Details of the truck seller.
- Warranties or certain assurances to minimize risk.

8. **Insurance**

Insurance is critical. Having an insurance quote for the truck indicates to the lenders that you're serious about buying it. This will likely improve your chances of getting the funds.

Small Business Administration(SBA) Loans

The Small Business Administration (SBA) partners with lenders on loans to small businesses. Notice that the SBA does not provide loans. What it does is set guidelines for loans offered by its lending partners to simplify access to funding while reducing risk for lenders.

Here are some benefits of loans backed up by the SBA:

- Some loans do not require collateral.

- You don't need to have large down payments.

- Competitive rates and fees.

- Some loan providers give business support to enhance your chances of success. If you think about it, this approach makes sense because the lender makes money when you succeed. It's a win-win situation.

- You're allowed to use the loan to buy long-term assets, such as trucks and buildings, and for operations.

The SBA loans start from as low as $500 to as high as $5.5 million. To access these loans, lenders look at several criteria, such as the following:

- The nature of the business and how it generates money.

- The kind of business ownership.

- The physical location of the business.

- The business must be registered and operating legally.

- You should be doing business and located in the U.S.

- The business owner must invest either sweat or cash equity in the company.

- The business is not allowed to source funds from any other lender.

As you can see, the requirements don't differ much from those of commercial trucking funding. If you prepare for your SBA funding as if you're going to apply for commercial truck financing, you'll improve your chances of success.

Business Line of Credit

A business line of credit works exactly like a personal credit card. It gives you access to revolving credit. This means that, if you qualify, you'll be allowed to borrow up to a specific limit. Once you have borrowed, you pay back the money, including interest. And then, you can again borrow from the total credit you have.

You don't have to borrow all the credit available. A positive thing about a business line of credit is that you pay interest only on your borrowed amount. This credit type suits short-term funding needs.

There are two types of business lines of credit. One kind is secured while the other is unsecured. The secured line of credit requires collateral. Typically, you'll use short-term assets, such as inventory as collateral. On the other hand, an unsecured line of credit tends to charge higher interest rates. To qualify, your business often should have a good track record and an unblemished credit profile.

To apply for a business line of credit is simple. All that is required is that you submit the following together with your application:

- Recent business bank statements.

- Tax returns.

- The latest financial statements.

- A business license.

Warning: The lender may call up the business line of credit anytime they want. At that point, you'll be asked to pay all the outstanding balance. Therefore, use the amount of credit that you know you'll be able to pay back on short notice.

Business Credit Card

A business credit card is designed specifically for company use. It is available for both small and large businesses. A credit card is an ideal tool to use if you want to build a business credit file.

Business credit card issuers may require backing through your personal guarantee. The way to apply for this credit card is the same as for a personal kind. You can get a business credit card from several institutions. Once again, shop around for better terms and interest rates. A 1% difference can make a massive difference in the amount of interest you pay.

Factoring

Factoring is a funding technique based on a business's future liquid assets like accounts receivable. This means that you can use assets like invoices to access funds on a short-term basis. Companies are willing to loan you money, at a fee, based on your liquid assets (excluding cash).

It is like these companies that buy your accounts receivable at a fee. The good thing is that they often pay you within 24 business hours after you deliver the load to the customer. Your customer then pays this sort of company from 30 to 35 days later.

The advantages of factoring include the ability for you to access money quickly. Also, you don't have to deal with individual customers about payments because you work with one factoring company. This saves you time for administration work. However, factoring can be costly because you may be charged from 3% to 5% of the load price, depending on its size.

If you decide to use a factoring company, choose one that is reputable and transparent with their fees and terms. You can obtain this information from other owner-operators who have been through the process before. Never sign any contract with a factoring company without studying it thoroughly. There may be something untoward in the contract which could land you into trouble later.

What's next now that you have a truck? It's time to run the trucking operations, and we tackle this topic next.

Chapter 5

Running Your Business

The manner in which you run your business determines its success or failure. So, you need ways to run your company successfully. And this begins with the right application of your business plan. It doesn't mean that you should follow the business plan to a tee even when things don't work. Your business plan serves as a starting point. And you'll tweak it where you deem necessary.

Hiring Reliable Truck Drivers

One of the most vital aspects of running a successful trucking business is to hire reliable and effective drivers. Even if you're an owner-operator, you still should hire a truck driver to swap time off. This would allow your truck to run more and make you more money. Furthermore, it's plain good business to have a relief driver because you need rest to be effective.

Finding good truck drivers in the United States isn't a walk in the park. The trucking industry suffers from one of the highest turnovers in the country. Smaller transporters have seen as high as a 73% driver turnover rate (Raphelson, 2018). So you need to have a water-tight recruiting process. Such a recruitment approach relies on thorough screening, hiring the right driver, followed by an effective orientation and onboarding process.

One tool to help in the driver hiring process is the Pre-Employment Screening Program (PSP) developed by the

FCMSA. The system offers access to a commercial driver's safety record kept in the FMCSA Motor Carrier Management Information System (MCMIS). The data you'll find gives you a driver safety record in the previous five years. These records include any crashes or inspections in which the driver was involved. The inspections go back up to three years. This gives you confidence that you're hiring someone with a higher chance of driving safely.

Driver Qualities to Look for When Hiring

Besides the safety record of a driver, there are other qualities to look for. As you know, a human being is complex and cannot be defined by a single variable. Hence, you need to check for a lot more when hiring a truck driver, including the following:

- **Reliability**: Every hiring person requires reliable employees. You are no exception. A reliable driver assures you that they'll do what they promise. You can trust that they'll deliver customer goods at the agreed times. If they encounter problems along the way, they'll raise a flag and let you know if there are changes to the original plan.

- **Self-reliant**: A truck driver who will always want your help isn't a good employee. You want someone who would own the truck, make tough decisions, and continuously update their relevant knowledge. This is the kind of driver who you know will solve problems when they pop up, and they will.

- **Stress management skills**: The trucking industry is tough and, therefore, requires a tough-minded truck driver. Such individuals have the ability to manage the stresses accompanying the driving job.

- **Fitness**: A fit body doesn't get sick easily. Furthermore, a fit driver is able to handle stressful situations better than an unfit one. Also, a fit driver can work for long hours and still stay alert and drive safely.

- **Top driving record**: A driver who possesses an impeccable driving record gives you confidence that your customers' goods and truck are safe. So, they tend to be cheaper to insure, which helps improve your trucking business's profitability.

Once you know what kind of a driver you're looking for, it's time to go out and find them.

Where to Find Truck Drivers

There are several ways of finding good truck drivers. The high turnover in the industry means some drivers are looking for companies that can take good care of them. Here are some approaches to use to search for drivers.

- **Networking**: Contact people you know, such as friends and family members, and let them know that you're looking for a truck driver. It also helps to inform them what kind of a driver you're looking for. It will save you time, energy, and making a recruitment mistake.

- **Online marketing**: This approach requires you to post your driver requirements on social media. You could also create valuable information and post it on your website to attract your kind of drivers. This is called content marketing. Other approaches include email marketing and pay-per-click advertising.

- **Post truck driver jobs on call-to-action channels, such as online job boards**. You may also run newspaper ads targeted to your kind of driver.

- **Contact potential drivers directly**. Some drivers post their resumes on job boards. You may collect their details and contact them directly to see if they have what you want.

Many other ways open up immediately when you begin the search for drivers. When matching a truck driver with your business, always check for the following:

- That they are comfortable being away from home and family frequently.

- That they don't mind working a variable schedule.

- You need to be indirect with this one. If you want to hire a driver for the long-term, be mindful that this aspect also depends on how you'll treat your driver. If you care for them, they'll likely care for you. We'll go deeper later when we talk about your retention strategy.

Truck Driver Salaries

Trucking companies often pay their drivers per mile covered. Different drivers get different wages based on experience, the kind of cargo they hail, qualifications, and where they drive. Standard rates start from $0.27 to $0.40 per mile (Roadmaster Drivers School, n.d.).

A typical driver covers anywhere from 2,000 to 3,000 miles per week. This means that you may expect to pay your drivers from $540 to $1,200 per week. However, keep in mind that the final amount will depend on your negotiations with the driver, as well as other benefits that you offer.

The good thing about paying per mile is that drivers push harder to cover more miles. They know that the more miles, the more money they'll make. Yours is to ensure that your drivers cover genuine and profitable miles.

How to Retain Your Truck Drivers

I've already alerted you on the high turnover in the trucking industry. Just imagine the impact a turnover like 94% has on large trucking companies. This means that you can spend a chunk of your time looking for drivers. And, after finding them, they leave within a short space of time. This is tragic. But you can improve your retention.

It starts with understanding why drivers change carriers so often. Then you can position yourself to be an employer of choice. And that process starts with recruitment. Hiring drivers that don't match your organizational culture is a sure means to a high driver turnover. That's not a good way of running a business because hiring and training drivers are costly. And, during the hiring process, you may not be able to use your full trucking capacity.

So, what should you include in your driver retention strategy? Here are five ways to keep drivers for longer.

1. **Respect and Appreciate Your Drivers**

   Most trucking businesses assume income and benefits can reduce driver attrition rates. If it were so, the problem of high driver turnover would have been nipped on the butt ages ago. So, there must be other factors involved.

   A 2019 Randall-Reilly truck driver poll discovered that 20% of truck drivers disliked their jobs because nobody appreciates what they do. In fact, they said that truck driving was a thankless job. Furthermore, 64% of them felt there isn't enough respect for truck drivers (Randall-Reilly & Commercial Carrier Journal, 2019).

   You can differentiate yourself by showing appreciation to all your employees all the time. It's even better if you make this part of your company DNA. One good way to show appreciation and respect is to prepare and send a weekly communiqué to your employees where you thank them for being part of your business.

2. **Set Achievable Job Expectations**

   A Stay Days Table index from Stay Metrics revealed that 64.9% of truck drivers hired in the first quarter of 2019 worked beyond 90 days (Commercial Carrier Journal, 2019). These drivers said that knowing what's expected of them was crucial in the first few days or weeks on the job.

   This means that, as a business owner, it's essential to inform your drivers, during recruitment, what their work schedule will be, their income, and the routes they'll travel. When you set these expectations, ensure that they're realistic to avoid drivers feeling like failures. Honestly, who wants to feel like a failure? I'm sure you and I don't, and we shouldn't expect others would like failing.

If you hire recruiters, tell them to be honest about the job and the company. Otherwise, when drivers find that what they were told isn't synonymous with what they see, they'll leave.

3. **Provide Driver Support**

The 2019 Randall-Reilly poll also found that 40% of drivers were concerned about government regulations and 37% worried about paying bills. Furthermore, drivers also rated spending time at home with family and their health as important.

These topics provide ample opportunity to write a weekly communiqué to your drivers and other employees. Your topics could include how drivers can stay healthy and explain how regulations benefit them and their families. As long as drivers see regulations as punishment, they're unlikely to comply, and this could hurt your business.

4. **Offer Attractive Pay**

When asked why trucking companies fail to attract drivers, 72% of the respondents in the Randall-Reilly poll said that transporters don't pay enough.

Concerning was that 37% said if offered more money elsewhere, they would leave for another fleet.

It shows how important pay is to truck drivers. And you cannot afford not to pay a competitive wage. You can do this by offering a respectable amount of regular and guaranteed mileage at a good pay per mile. Also, you could offer health and retirement packages to reduce financial weight on your drivers.

5. **Introduce Driver-Benefit Technology**

   Technology, like dash cams, can help improve driver productivity and safety. Of course, drivers, like everyone else, like to be trusted. Unfortunately, technology like this could make drivers feel like they're not trusted.

   So, install technology that provides drivers with clear benefits and make that a reason for its use. But do ensure that this technology improves productivity at the same time. That way, you have a technology that delivers a win-win for both company and driver.

A good example is installing satellite T.V. and radio. These gadgets entertain your drivers and can help them reduce stress. Less stress means better problem-solving and, therefore, better performance. And improved performance makes your business profitable.

The Need for Other Employees

Life has a way of getting in the way. You may face life's curveballs and that may stop the operation of your business in your absence. You may also want to grow your business, and it won't be possible if you're all alone in the company.

So, you may need to hire other employees to help with a variety of business tasks. Yes, you may decide to outsource some tasks like legal or bookkeeping, but you may not have the time to hold these third parties accountable in the event they don't deliver proper work. For this reason, hire at least one other employee to help you answer phones and handle your business records, such as accounting.

The way you hire any employee involves implementing savvy recruitment strategies. Hire them like you are looking for a business partner. Aren't they your business partner? They are because their livelihood will depend on the success of your business.

How to Find Paying Customers

If there's any most important task in your business, it is to find paying customers. This is so for a good reason. Customers are the lifeblood of any trucking business. There's no cash flow without customers. To keep having customers and positive cash flow, it is helpful to diversify.

It's important to solicit customers who pay high rates per load. This helps your business become profitable without having to cover thousands and thousands of miles. But finding customers can be tough, not only for trucking businesses but for any business. Your ability to find good-paying loads will determine your business's success or failure.

At this point, you would have given thought to who your ideal customer is when creating your business plan. What's left is to take action and find them. But how will you find them? We'll get to that in a moment. Let's first look at what kind of a shipper is the right customer for a trucking company.

This criterion is general in nature. Yours would be more specific but cover these qualifications as well. Here's what to look for in an idea shipper: They pay well and on time. The shipper supplies loads regularly. They're an established and reputable shipper. The customer offers loads that match your freight lanes.

Armed with that customer information, you head out to look for them using one or more of the following ways.

Six Ways of Finding Customers

It's now time to find customers who will bring revenue to your business. There are several ways of doing this. But we'll go over seven powerful ones here.

1. **Networking at Industry Associations**

   To access members of industry associations often requires you to join the organization. It's not every association that has your customer. Choose industry associations you know your ideal customers belong to. For example, if your customer is in retail, then look at joining retail associations. If in contraction, you join construction associations and so on.

   Some industry associations welcome corporate members. You can use this opportunity to join and network with your ideal shippers. In the process, you'll be able to see how you can serve them. Your big idea is not to sell your services but to collect connections and leads. Business leads are people you can potentially serve. Don't try to sell because the environment isn't conducive to deals involving large sums of money. Consultative selling is a better approach to getting trucking business.

Consider creating an industry report beneficial to your ideal customers. Then you can offer it to your customers in exchange for their contact details. That way, you add value to them and their business immediately. Furthermore, this approach sets you apart from your competitors and establishes you as an authority.

Later, get in touch with your newly-acquired contacts to set up meetings where you'll sell them your services.

Another option is to get a list of members of a given association. Then send the members your report to establish the first contact. A few days later, you may contact them to check if they received the report. That then provides you an easy start to a selling process. The standard rate directory service list book also provides an option to obtain lists of your targeted associations' lists.

2. **Register with Government as a Contractor**

The government hires many small businesses for various services and products. You can access regular work from the government, and they're often reliable on payments. With many government departments and agencies, there are ample opportunities to provide a trucking service.

What you need to do is register with the government as a vendor. Search for relevant business opportunities using keywords and other criteria like locations. Then review selected opportunities to understand what the government wants and what their terms are.

If you are interested in a job, all you do is prepare a bid at competitive prices while staying profitable. Finally, submit your bid and wait for the decision on who gets awarded the contract.

It's advisable to start bidding for government work at the local level. This will help you understand the government's procurement processes, so you become efficient and bidding and project delivery. If you get a larger contract, you may have to source extra funding to be able to complete the job in time. But this is an easier problem to solve because you can request funds from factoring companies.

3. **Hire a Freight Broker**

Freight brokers connect shippers to carriers and make money in the process. Getting the services of a broker is a good strategy for a trucking business start up. They do most of the work, such as negotiating rates with shippers.

However, you should be aware that you'll likely be paid lower rates than directly working shippers. Still, ensure that they pay you more than your cost per mile. And ensure that there are no hidden fees by studying the contract thoroughly.

4. **Use Truck Dispatcher Services**

There are freight dispatchers that also offer load finding services to trucking companies. They charge either a fixed amount or on a pay per load basis. This option suits startup businesses like yours because you don't have a profitable list of clients yet.

5. **Online Marketing**

Online marketing refers to initiatives you do online to get paying customers. There are many ways to do online marketing, including content marketing, email marketing, pay-per-click advertising, and social media marketing. If you don't have online marketing skills, don't jump into using them because you could make costly mistakes. First, familiarize yourself with your chosen online marketing approach to avoid losing time and money.

6. **Use Load Boards**

We've spoken about this when working out what to quote brokers and shippers. In the beginning, opt for free load boards if you can't afford paid versions.

7. **Personal Prospecting**

Personal prospecting involves conducting research to find shippers in your location. Then, you check what kind of goods they ship and to where. If they carry cargo that runs on your lane, you get in touch them and ask for a short meeting over coffee or lunch.

In the meeting, focus on asking questions about their business. Begin with the general and drive to the specifics relating to shipping. In the process, you'll discover how your business could be of better service to them.

Don't use all the above techniques to find customers. Select two or three, and work them. You're welcome to swap one with another if it doesn't deliver the results you want. However, remember to be patient.

How to Price Your Freight

It costs money to transport cargo from one point to the next. You cannot afford to transport the load at a higher cost than the pay you receive. It's impossible to build a thriving business that way. A trucking business should be able to fund itself with the cargo that it transports.

Therefore, to run a profitable trucking business requires that you know your revenue and expenses. Here's how to figure out your cost per mile.

1. **Compute the Total Mileage**

   The mileage a truck covers determines how much the shipper pays for a given type of load. Different truck drivers cover varied mileages per month. These mileages include both paid and unpaid (called deadhead) distances. The average truck driver covers about 8,400 miles a month. I'll use this figure to illustrate our calculations as I proceed with working out the cost per mile.

2. **Determine Your Fixed Expenses**

   The business costs that you'll incur fall into either the fixed or variable expense category. Fixed costs stay the same from one month to the next irrespective of the amount of work you do. For example, monthly license fees and truck payments stay unchanged.

   Some fixed costs get paid annually and therefore should be distributed monthly for our purposes here. Let's assume that the cost of a given permit is $1,800 per year. That works out to $150 per month ($1,800/12).

3. **Compute Your Variable Expenses**

   Unlike fixed costs, variable expenses often change monthly. The actual amount due to a variable cost depends on the mileage you drive. When you cover a large distance, the cost will be higher and vice versa. Examples of variable costs include fuel, maintenance, and meal expenses.

Suppose your fuel cost is $0.55 per mile. Over a month when you cover 8,400 miles, you'll spend $4,620 ($0.55 x 8,400) on fuel. In a month when the truck drives 6,300, the fuel cost works out to $3,465.

4. **Figure Out the Cost Per Mile**

Now, divide the total fixed cost by 8,400 to find the fixed expenses per mile. For example, if your total fixed cost is $5,620, then the fixed expense per mile will be $0.67 ($5,620/8,400).

Using the same approach, calculate your variable cost per mile. A total variable cost of $2,350 leads to $0.28 per mile.

To determine the total cost per mile, simply add the fixed cost per mile to the variable expenses per mile. The total cost per mile is $0.95 ($0.67 + $0.28) in the example used above.

Alternatively, you can add the total fixed and variable costs and divide the outcome by 8,400 like this: $7,970 ($5,620 + $2,350) divided by 8,400 to get $0.95. This means that you cannot quote below $0.95 per mile per load and still be profitable. To make your calculations easy, use this **spreadsheet**. All you do is insert appropriate numbers in the spreadsheet and it will effortlessly compute the cost per mile for you. But there's more to consider in your pricing.

What Else to Include in Your Pricing

A freight delivery cost depends on three components, namely, linehaul, fuel surcharge, and accessorials. Let's go over each so you can have a better understanding of these terms.

- **Linehaul**: This is the cost to carry a shipment from its origin to the destination. The distance covered determines the total expense. The calculation we did above was linehaul. Linehaul for LTL and parcels varies based on the weight or volume the load occupies in the trailer. The larger the weight or volume, the more the linehaul.

- **Fuel surcharge**: When a trucker buys fuel, they get charged fuel tax. So, truckers include an additional fuel charge in their prices to hedge against diesel fuel fluctuations. This extra fuel charge is called the fuel surcharge.

  Fuel surcharge can be added either as a percentage of the linehaul cost of cost per mile. Truckers use fuel data from the weekly (on Tuesdays) updated U.S. Energy Information (EIA) website.

- **Accessorials**: Beginner truckers often make the mistake of excluding accessorials in the load prices. These are charges added to the shipment cost for any extra work or time the trucker puts into the shipment, often excluded in the originally agreed price.

Three Shipment Pricing Methods

There are three shipment pricing methods depending on the work to be done and the trucker's preference. The choice of pricing method affects the loading costs. The methods include spot, contract, and project pricing.

1. **Spot Pricing**

   Spot pricing is a method where negotiated prices depend on trucks and loads' current supply and demand. As a result, this pricing method is volatile. You can use this type to fill up trucking capacity to avoid deadhead miles or idle vehicles.

2. **Contract Pricing**

   Contract prices are shipment costs based on future volumes and shipper requirements. The price often stays the same over a twelve-month period. But bear mind that there is no guarantee you'll carry loads daily. So, it's essential to have multiple contracts to increase the utilization of your freight capacity.

   The agreement between the shipper and carrier provides for loading when the trucker has capacity.

3. **Project Pricing**

   Finally, there is project pricing, where negotiated prices follow the contract approach. However, project prices are valid for shorter periods.

Pricing Strategies in the Trucking Industry

The competition for loads is tight in the trucking industry. With increasing transportation costs, it's essential to use profitable pricing strategies to become and stay profitable. Successful trucking businesses tend to have similar pricing strategies. For example, they charge freight prices commensurate with the value of their services and products.

So, you must commit to profitable pricing approaches if you want to be profitable. Most importantly, never allow sales representatives (if you have any) to adjust your prices.

You can either use static or dynamic pricing. Dynamic pricing gives a price advantage. The change in prices comes from altering delivery areas; the products delivered, varying demand, and the economic environment. This approach allows you to tailor your prices to stay profitable. Let's go over three variations of dynamic pricing.

1. **Revenue Management Pricing**

   Revenue management pricing is common with less-than-truckload (LTL) truckers. Prices reflect destinations and optimization based on the proportion of a truckload occupied by the shipper's load.

   This strategy allows shippers to price their services based on full truckload irrespective of their product occupies' space.

2. **Yield Management Pricing**

   The yield management pricing strategy sets prices to reflect the need for quick and timely delivery of freight.

This approach works well for carriers who transport perishable products.

The quoted prices take into account changing established routes and swapping drivers to meet the delivery time requirement.

3. **Geographic Pricing**

In geographic pricing, the prices mirror changes in fuel costs, the truck's wear and tear, and the driver's wages. Long-haul companies favor this kind of pricing because they can optimize their revenue.

A popular example of utilizing this approach is called zone pricing. Here, prices differ based on geographic locations, that is, distance from shipping point to destination.

Those are the main approaches to dynamic pricing you could use. However, you may opt to do uniform pricing. This strategy applies the same prices for all shippers. Although less common, short-haul and local delivering companies use it.

Four Tips to Negotiate Freight Rates

Would you like to get the best rates on load boards? How would you like to know a technique that helps swell your company's bottom line? Whether you're new in the trucking industry or are a new owner-operator, you should negotiate freight rates.

The keyword is 'negotiate.' Why? Because not all loads, especially those on load boards, include added transport fees like accessorials. Also, freight brokers may give themselves way higher markups and hurt you in the process.

Savvy negotiations require preparation and knowledge. Here are four ideas to consider when you plan to negotiate freight rates.

1. Understand Your Operating Costs

Your operating cost is the expense you pay to haul a load for one mile. We've covered how to compute this figure earlier in the book. As we said, this figure is crucial because you can't run a profitable business unless your freight loads pay more than your cost per mile.

Importantly, knowing your cost per mile allows you to set negotiation limits on freight rates to accept. Additionally, your cost per mile gives you an indication of where to anchor your freight prices. Anchoring is a process of setting a price's frame of reference. The higher, but reasonable, the anchoring price, the greater the chance of getting a larger price.

2. Check Load Rates for Round-Trips

Certain areas pay low freight rates. For example, freights to Florida often pay well. But the return journeys don't pay good rates. Armed with this knowledge, you can negotiate higher round-trip rates instead of focusing only on individual lanes. Although this approach is uncommon, it gives you the opportunity to avoid deadhead.

If you can't have a round-trip, then negotiate a higher rate to a destination and opt for a breakeven return leg to stay profitable. But try to avoid taking frequent low-paying lanes because it's a habit that can hurt your business severely.

3. **Select Loads with High Load-to-Truck Ratios**

A high load-to-truck ratio signifies that the demand for trucks is high relative to available loads. This provides you with room for negotiating prices as opposed to a low truck-to-load rate. Shippers become desperate to have their loads delivered. This is good for your trucking business.

4. **Notice the Load's Times**

Sometimes loads stay on the load board for long periods. This may cause shippers or brokers to start getting anxious and frustrated. This is the exact time when you chip in and offer your trucks.

The way to get these opportunities is to note the times loads spend on the load boards. When you see a particular load staying on the board for far too long, you call the shipper or broker and make yourself available to take it. That's when negotiations will begin.

The shorter the window is to pick-up time, the more shippers and brokers fret and are willing to negotiate. The hours of work for truck drivers combined with load timings provide a ripe chance to negotiate better freight rates.

When you negotiate, try to ask as many questions around the load as possible. The more the shipper or broker speaks, the more chance they give you to spot weaknesses and opportunities to argue for higher rates.

Not many business owners are fond of negotiating. This gives you an unfair advantage if you make up your mind to make negotiating part of your business strategy. Negotiating isn't a life and death action. The worst thing that can happen is hearing a 'no.' And when you hear this little word, you simply move back to the load board and other freight sources.

Once the negotiations reach their conclusion, ensure that you get agreed rates (including surcharges) and terms in writing before taking the load. This will help you avoid costly misunderstandings later on. Most important, before you load, do credit checks on the broker or shipper to eliminate the chance of working with bogus people and companies.

Scheduling and Fleet Management

Running a fleet effectively requires you to manage driver scheduling, truck maintenance and associated records, and driver training plans. You have two options available for this important task. You may choose to do it manually or through a fleet management software. The latter offers an easier and more efficient approach to fleet management and it's the approach I recommend.

Once set up, fleet management software provides ways to print copies of various reports for filing as required by various regulations such as IFTA taxes. You don't have to enter every data point and do calculations manually. The system works its computing magic in the background. And all you do is feed it a few numbers from which these different reports will be created.

Using this system allows you to optimize route plans and deliver freights on time. As you can tell, fleet management software helps minimize operational expense, improve driver productivity, and jerk up your business's profitability.

How Many Hours Should Truck Drivers Work?

Truck drivers aren't allowed to drive for as long as they want because it can be unsafe for themselves and other road users. So, some laws and regulations help ensure truck drivers work a given amount of time.

The FMCSA sets the hours of work for truck drivers. Interstate driving is subject to federal regulations. Here are some of those regulations that truck drivers should adhere to:

- Truck drivers are allowed to work only 60 hours over seven successive days or 70 hours over an eight-day duration. To manage these hours, a driver must keep a log for seven days and eight days thereafter.

- Drivers are allowed to work for up to 14 hours after being off duty for 10 hours. Of the 14 hours, 11 must be for driving.

- A driver must get a 30-minute break eight hours after coming on duty.

- Breaks, meals, and fuel stops are excluded in the 14-hour duration.

However, there's an Adverse Driving Condition exception that gives drivers an additional two hours of driving. This happens provided the driver experiences traffic delays due to construction, adverse weather, and traffic incidents.

There's also a 16-hour exception rule that applies to drivers on a one-day work schedule. Such drivers are allowed to work for 16 hours if they start and end their work at the same terminal.

Penalties for Violating Hours of Service (HOS) Rules

Like any government rule, a truck driver or transporter gets punished for violating the hours of service. The severity of the penalty or fine will depend on the kind and seriousness of the offense. Here's what may happen when a driver breaks the working hours rules:

- If your drivers work beyond allowable hours, they may be stopped by the roadside until they accumulate enough of a rest period to comply once more. State and local relevant officials may assess applicable fines.

- FMCSA may penalize your business and driver a fee ranging from $1,000 to $11,000 per infringement based on the severity of the violation.

- Your company's safety rating may be downgraded if you rack up a pattern of violations.

- The Federal law enforcement officials can charge you civil penalties if they find you knowingly allowed the infringement. The same could apply to your drivers.

Other Government Regulations to Comply With

There are other government regulations that your business should adhere to for trouble-free trucking. Let's talk about four important ones.

1. **Drug Testing**

   It's mandatory to test truck drivers for drugs and alcohol. Any driver who tests positive (verified) must be removed from their work immediately. If found adulterated, they should suffer the same consequences. A driver who refuses drug and alcohol testing must be removed from safety-sensitive tasks.

   A trucking company must report its drug testing results to the government.

2. **Engine Idling**

   Strange as it may sound, not all states and municipalities allow drivers to idle their engines.

   Some who do allow engine idling give drivers a few minutes. Running the engine beyond that period may attract fines up to $25,000 (Trucking Job Finder, n.d.).

3. **Weight Limit**

   Heavy vehicles can damage public roads faster than their lighter counterparts. For this reason, states and cities place a weight limit on trucks that carry cargo. So, it's important to familiarize yourself with these limits to avoid fines and penalties.

   Usually, a truck found to be over the weight limits while carrying cargo may be stopped until another trailer reduces the load. This, obviously, will delay your truck and affect your profitability.

4. **Safety Audits**

The government requires truck companies to undergo a safety audit in the first 12 months of starting their operations. So, your business must avail itself for this audit or risk the FMCSA revoking their registration. This is because the safety audit is part of the process of getting a permanent operating authority.

Technology to Include in Your Truck

Certain technological devices help your drivers and company to comply with government rules and regulations. I'll discuss with you two of them.

- **Electronic logging device (ELD)**: An ELD is a device to track a driver's driving time and record duty status. As I explained earlier, you need to track your driver's hours of service. And this instrument ensures that you comply with the U.S. ELD mandate.

  The ELD you choose must be registered with and self-certified with the FMCSA. The ultimate goal of the ELD is to assist in creating a safer work environment for drivers.

  Additionally, an ELD simplifies fleet management.

  - **Global Positioning System (GPS)**: A GPS is a device that helps you monitor the speed your trucks travel while on the road. As you know, a high speed increases the chances of accidents.

A GPS may influence your drivers to drive at the right speeds. But you should be careful about using the GPS to monitor your trucks' speeds because drivers dislike being micromanaged.

- **Cam dash**: A dash camera helps drivers improve visibility and potentially reduce driving incidents. Therefore, it lowers the cost associated with truck accidents. If involved in a truck accident, the cam dash may exonerate your driver with video footage. Also, a cam dash simplifies insurance claims.

Truck Maintenance

Well-maintained trucks can help your driver stay safe while lowering operating costs. As a result, maintaining your trucks is a way to improve the profitability of your business. Here are some maintenance tasks you should do on your trucks.

Do regular engine oil and filter changes. If possible, replace the filter with the type recommended by the manufacturer. A quick check into the truck's user manual should furnish you with the frequency of oil and filter changes.

Check engine coolant, power steering fluid, windshield washer, and brake fluid level prior to taking a journey.

Regularly rotate your tires to avoid uneven wear. This

also helps to lengthen the service the tires give you.

Inspect the exterior of the truck for any signs of damage.

Acquire the services of an expert to inspect your trucks at least annually.

Check to ensure the temperature control unit's proper functioning, accuracy and calibration of the temperature monitoring instruments.

Inspect the insulation, floor grooves, and drains.

Check proper operation of the interior and exterior lights, mirrors, brakes, battery, and steering.

With a sound truck, you could see more life and performance from it.

Join Trucking Associations

Joining trucking associations has different benefits than becoming a member of your customer associations. You join trucking associations to become updated with developments within the industry and regulatory changes. In addition, you also expand your network, an important resource for building a trucking business.

One of the organizations to consider joining is the American Trucking Association. One of its main reasons for existence is to help members operate safely while being profitable. Besides staying current with industry developments, you'll access business growth initiatives like conferences and education.

Take time and research trucking associations that you can join at the state level. Also, consider joining specialized associations such as the Truckload Carriers Association.

Alright. That brings us to the end of running your business. Now, let's turn our attention to managing your business's finances, a crucial part of running a thriving trucking business.

Chapter 6
Managing Your Business's Finances

It may be a cliché but the following idea carries power if you run a successful trucking business. That idea is this: you cannot manage it if you can't measure it. This thought also applies to managing your business finances. Therefore, it is imperative to determine early on what you'll measure to ensure your business succeeds. Fortunately, others have already walked this path. This means that you don't have to reinvent the wheel but simply learn what they've measured to manage a business's finances. I'll take you through the things involved in business accounting and financial management in a moment.

First, let's go over the process you need to follow to build an emergency fund. We talked earlier in the book about the value of having an emergency. Now, let's build it.

A Business Emergency Fund

As the name suggests, an emergency fund serves to finance your business costs in case there's an emergency. It follows that you should define events that fall into the emergency category. By definition, an emergency is an unforeseen occurrence often unprepared for things like a fire that licks your truck. Or your truck's refrigeration unit breaking down unexpectedly. Normally, an emergency in your trucking business can stop the operations.

Some businesses elect to use either a credit card or business line of credit to fund such emergencies. That's fine as long as they pay them before their bankers add interest. But if they wait until after the addition of interest, they end up overpaying and reducing their businesses' profitability, and this isn't good business management.

To avoid this difficult situation, why not create an emergency fund? When faced with an emergency, you simply whip out your debit card and pay for your refrigeration unit's repairs. The good thing with having cash is that you can negotiate lower costs far easier than using a credit line. Thus, your business profitability stays unaffected. And you experience less stress, a good thing for a business.

How to Build an Emergency Fund

Like anything else, creating and building an emergency fund takes initiative and the willingness to sacrifice. Most importantly, you should set it as a goal achievable within a given time period. Here are the steps, in sequence, to take to build an emergency fund.

1. **Set the goal amount you need to accumulate**. The amount of your emergency fund should cover three to six months of your business expenses. The time period provides you with ample time to return to normal operations. This means that if you spend $7,500 per month, your emergency fund should be between $22,500 (3 x $7,500) and $45,000 (6 x $7,500).

These numbers may seem large, and they are. That's why when you have this fund you can have peace of mind. Remember that you're going to build this fund like building a house. You're going to take it one step at a time like we're doing now.

I'll use the lower figure of $22,500 to illustrate the process as we proceed. In other words, the emergency fund goal is to save $22,500.

2. **Decide on the target date to have set up the fund**. Setting a target date adds a bit of urgency. It works like a deadline to complete a task. When there's no deadline, what does a person normally do? Procrastinate, isn't it? And setting a target date eliminates this tendency to delay taking action.

   For our purpose, I'll take it we're going to finish building this fund in 12 months. There's something else we're going to use this period for. It's going to help us figure out how much to set aside monthly.

3. **Work out how much to save monthly**. This is simple to do. Take your target emergency fund and divide it by the period to build the fund. In this case, I take $22,500 and divide it by 12. And the outcome is $1,875. This means that the business should put aside, in a special fund, $1,875 monthly for emergency purposes.

   Before we talk about where to get the money to save, let me address this question, "What happens if the business faces an emergency while still building the fund?" Well, to be frank, you use the money that's available. It is the cheapest money you'll ever have to handle financial emergencies. But that means you'll have to start afresh from there and rebuild the fund.

Alright. Let's carry on with an emergency fund-building process.

4. **Spend less than the business makes**. This isn't easy, especially if you aren't getting better freight rates. You should because if you don't, your business stands a small chance of succeeding.

    Other ways to save costs include buying fuel at lower prices. I'll explain how to do this later in this chapter. Another option is to negotiate almost every business expense you incur. Any saving you make goes into the emergency fund.

5. **Earn more money**. When earning more money, you should keep your fixed costs the same. Thus, you'll be able to build a larger cushion between your income and expenses and save more. This requires discipline. It's hard, but the rewards, as often said, are worth it.

    Ways to earn more money include getting more profitable loads. The way to do this is by chasing after high-paying freight. It may not be that easy. But committing to building the emergency fund forces you to push hard to obtain those high-paying loads.

That's all there is to building an emergency fund. As you can see, it requires you to manage your finances while getting paying customers. Let's go ahead and look at the actual task of managing your business's finances.

Business Accounting

The mark of a successful trucking business is how well the owner keeps financial and operational numbers. It's like keeping a business scorecard. This means that the numbers will inform you whether you're winning or losing. You could then make informed decisions that help you stay on track to achieve your business goals.

Business accounting involves capturing financial numbers that feed a variety of reports. These reports are called financial statements, and they serve a variety of functions. I'll get to them in a moment.

There are important accounting terms that you should be familiar with. Let's go over them briefly.

1. **Assets**: An business asset is something that a business owns. It can be physical or intellectual. Some common assets are buildings, trucks, cash in the bank, and inventory.

2. **Liabilities**: A business liability is anything that your company owes. In short, a liability is a debt. Good examples of liabilities are a truck loan and taxes.

3. **Equity**: An equity is what remains when the value of liabilities is taken out of the value of assets. In formula form, here's how accountants represent it:

    Equity = Assets - Liabilities

As the equation suggests, when the value of liabilities exceeds that of the assets, you have negative equity. It means that the business owes someone. This is not a good space to be in.

As a business owner, you'll have a share of your company's ownership. If you are the sole owner, then all the business equity is yours. But if you own 60% of the business, then your equity is also 60%.

4. **Revenue**: When a business trades, it makes money. All that cash that comes into the business is termed revenue or gross revenue. Accountants often report revenue generated over a given period, such as monthly, half-yearly, or annually.

5. **Gains**: At times, you may sell some of your assets to generate quick cash. This income will result in a one-time increase in gross revenue. Such income is called a gain.

6. **Expenses**: This is self-explanatory, isn't it? An expense is a cost that the business incurs to run its operations.

7. **Losses**: Sometimes, you may sell a business asset at a cost less than the price you paid to acquire it. The difference between these two numbers is called losses.

The terms above are critical when analyzing financial statements. And it's essential to know the purpose of each of these financial statements. You cannot manage the finances of a business without using these vital reports. A simple search online can give you access to templates for preparing each of these major financial statements. Here's a short introduction to each of the main financial statements.

1. **Balance sheet**: A balance sheet is also called a statement of financial position. It gives the financial standing of a business at a particular point in time. Businesses use this statement to capture their assets, liabilities, and equity. Its main job is to show you the overall health of your business.

2. **Income statement**: This statement reports on the income the business generates as well as the expenses. It usually covers a given period, such as monthly, quarterly, or annually. This means that if you want to know whether your business is profitable or not, you use the income statement.

3. **Cash flow statement**: A cash flow statement captures the amount of cash the business possesses and projects future money movements (cash flows). It shows the day-to-day financial health of a business. It's a key statement because, without readily available cash, a business can battle to pay operational expenses. And if a business runs out of cash, it may fail despite the income statement showing a profit.

Those are the three major financial statements that you should be able to read and understand. Above all, you should be able to use them to make savvy business decisions.

Now, armed with the knowledge of key accounting terms and financial statements, you need to know the actions to take to generate their numbers. That's an important job. As you know, the kind of financial data you gather will determine the usefulness of your financial statements.

Capturing financial numbers can be done in one of two ways. You may choose to do it manually or through accounting software. I'm not a fan of manually creating financial statements because it takes time and is prone to errors. Instead, I prefer using an accounting system that requires punching in a few numbers and letting the technology do its magic behind the scenes. This saves time and allows you to focus on your core operations, like finding better paying freight loads.

An accounting system ideally suits a startup because you can easily run your business without accounting personnel or an accounting department. What's key is selecting the right accounting system. What do I mean by an accounting system? Let me explain.

You can run your business accounting functions based on either the accrual or cash-based system. The difference between the two systems is the timing of when the business receives cash. A cash-based system records income when the business receives money. Expenses get logged only when cash leaves the company. This system suits simple operations, such as for a small business where tracking of cash flow is vital.

In contrast, an accrual system captures revenue when the business earns it even if the money is not yet in the bank. For example, immediately you deliver a shipper's load, the price the customer should pay gets recorded as revenue. The same applies to expenses. They get logged into the system even before the actual cash exits the company. This system often works well for large corporations with resources to handle its complexity.

For the accounting system you choose to use to be effective, you'll regularly maintain your books. You want to feed the necessary numbers, if possible, daily or as soon as you have them. And it should be easy when you use accounting software because you enter a few numbers. This helps keep your financial numbers up to date and allow you to know on a daily basis where your business is going.

Any receipts you get should be kept safe for the IRS and state fuel tax purposes. One cool idea is to make digital copies of the receipts and keep them into your computer. Don't forget to regularly backup your computer to avoid loss of your business data due to things like theft or fire.

Monitoring Business Expenses

As we've discussed earlier in this book, your business has fixed costs such as truck payments, loan payments, payroll, and truck insurance. I also made you aware of the importance of determining your cost per mile. Doing this required not only the fixed costs but also your variable expenses. The numbers that you generated in this process form your operating budget. You may already know from your personal life that a budget is crucial for financial success. So it is for a small business like yours.

Your budget is the baseline from which to measure the effectiveness of your business financial management tasks. You should know whether you're running your company on a budget, below budget, or above budget over a given period.

One of the major expenses that can result in the above budget operations is fuel costs. It's not unusual to spend $4,000 per month on diesel (CDL.com, n.d.). As you already know, fuel cost is but one of the variable expenses. Others include tires and truck maintenance. The main reason for monitoring each of your expenses is to ensure your business stays profitable.

Since fuel costs make up a major portion of your business budget, it's necessary to discuss it in detail. Unlike regular drivers, truck drivers pay fuel taxes on the diesel they buy and use in each state. And the cheapest diesel is not based on the pump price. So, you need to understand how fuel prices and taxes work to come up with a cost-effective fuel-buying strategy. Not only will this strategy help you buy fuel cost-effectively, but it can also guide your route planning.

What's the Best Fuel-Buying Strategy?

The buying of fuel for trucks can be confusing to new truck owners. Ridding this confusion requires an understanding of how fuel pricing works.

Each state charges a different price and tax for fuel. IFTA requires you to pay tax to each state you drive through, irrespective of where you buy the fuel. So, you pay for the fuel used in each of the jurisdictions you drove through. To simplify this process, let me show you how the IFTA taxes get calculated.

How to Calculate IFTA Taxes

To do this exercise, all you need are your fuel receipts, state to state miles you traveled, and current IFTA rates obtainable on their website. Armed with this information, this is what you do, step by step.

1. Compute the total mileage you covered during the reporting quarter. All you do is add the mileages covered in each state together. Your GPS or ELD can furnish you with this data.

2. Add up the gallons of fuel from your receipts to obtain the total you used during the quarter.

3. Determine the miles you covered per gallon of fuel. Simply divide the answer from step 1 by the answer from step 2 above.

4. Now, for each state, work out the gallons that you burned in that state. Simply multiply the answer in step 3 above by the mileage you covered in a state. You do this calculation for each state you traveled through during the reporting quarter.

5. Calculate, using the latest IFTA rates, the fuel tax to pay for each state. All you do is multiply the answer in step 4 above by the IFTA tax rate for that state.

6. Now, compute the tax you've already paid to each state when fueling your truck. This requires multiplying the total fuel bought in the state by the state's IFTA tax rate.

7. Calculate the amount of fuel tax you owe in each state by subtracting the answer in step 6 from the answer in step 5 above. Some taxes will be negative while others

positive. Your total IFTA tax is the sum of the fuel tax for each state.

8. Finally, you do the IFTA tax filing.

That's all there is to the process of figuring out the amount of IFTA tax to pay.

Because of the different state fuel taxes, you cannot use pump prices to tell which jurisdiction sells diesel cheaper. Instead, you must work out the base price of fuel per state. By the way, the base price is simply the difference between pump price and fuel tax. For example, let's say the diesel price in Colorado is $2.174 and the fuel tax rate is $0.2050 for each gallon you buy, respectively. Then, the base price will be $2.174 minus $0.2050 which equals $1.969 a gallon. This latter price we've figured out is the base diesel price in Colorado.

So, it's important to know the states that you'll pass through when you deliver your freight. Then, work out the state that charges the lowest base price. Once done, you can plan your routes so buy diesel in that state.

There is another way you could pay lower fuel prices.

Use Reward Cards

Rewards cards are credit cards that offer fuel rewards when you fill fuel at a gas station. Some reward cards can offer you 3% cashback when you buy fuel at given gas stations. This means that if you buy fuel worth $500, you'd be rewarded with $15 cashback. This may not sound like much. But if you spend $4,000 on fuel a month, you could get back as much as $120 to use for things like building an emergency fund.

Why It's Essential to Eliminate Deadhead Miles

Deadhead miles refer to the distance you cover with an empty truck. The problem with this is that you still incur operating costs while no money comes into the business. So, deadhead miles are like somebody stealing money from your business. The trucking industry sees average deadhead miles of about 35% (Dalloo, 2019). Another problem with deadhead miles is that the truck is two and half times more likely to be involved in an accident tan with freight (Payne, 2016).

To avoid driving at a loss, deadhead miles might push you to charge higher freight rates. As such, you may not become deadhead miles price competitive and potentially lose customers. So, you need to have a strategy to circumvent deadhead miles.

One way is to use technology to your advantage. These tools help you match loads on a driver's route to eliminate deadhead miles. Other actions you may take include the following:

- Planning your loads ahead of time.

- Staying on schedule barring unforeseen circumstances. But even with this challenge, you could still communicate with shippers so that they could accommodate you.

- Bundle lanes with low and high volumes and offer shippers a discount. Try to at least get a higher freight rate than your cost per mile.

Running an Effective Collection Strategy

The trucking industry isn't a cash-based market. Instead, you deliver the freight, send an invoice, and get paid in 30, 60, or, in some extreme situations, 90 days. This means that you need to become skilled in cash collection. And that requires you to have a functional and effective collection strategy.

An ineffective strategy could result in cash flow problems, one of the major causes of business failures. With a sure-to-get-cash collection strategy, you'll free yourself to focus your energies on your core business of shipping loads. But a collection strategy doesn't work in isolation. It requires you to have sound contracts that specify exactly when the payment for the load is to be made. Furthermore, you should send clear and complete invoices with instructions on how your customers should pay you.

Here's what to consider when creating an effective collection strategy.

- **Run credit checks on your customers**. Doing this helps you to work with honest and reliable customers. All it requires is for you to run credit and background checks through inexpensive online services.

- **Create an invoice tracking system**. A system like this enables you to quickly detect overdue payments and act swiftly. Some systems are software-based. It's safer and cheaper to try free versions at the start of your business and upgrade as and when the need arises. If you want, you may start with a simple spreadsheet and build a few formulas to highlight invoices at different stages with specific color codes.

- **Eliminate prolonging payment terms**. Where possible, keep payments to 30 days during tough economic times. Offering an incentive like a discount could influence your customers to pay early. But ensure that you don't lose money in the process.

- **Invoice your customers as soon as you deliver the load**. There are invoicing apps that you can populate as soon as you deliver your customer's freight. This avoids payment excuses from some customers.

Now, after you get paid, you would like to access the funds as soon as possible. The way to do this is by signing up for functionalities like direct deposits or automated clearing house (ACH) transfers.

At times, it may become hard to access your cash when you desperately want it. As I explained earlier in the book, you could use any of the following avenues to access cash on short notice:

- Factoring.
- Business line of credit.
- Short-term loans.
- Business credit card.

However, use these sources sparingly because borrowing costs money, which, in turn, will affect your business profitability.

Instead put more effort and time into your collection strategy as best as you can.

This chapter completes all that you need to know to start and build a thriving trucking business. The next section provides you with key ideas covered throughout the book.

Conclusion

Sometimes we read books and quickly forget the information and ideas that we got from them. That's why some people often read a book three, four, or five times. While reading a book, you find content and ideas that you know are useful. As a business consultant, I'm fortunate to understand what key concepts you may need to remind yourself about. And I included them in this chapter. The reason is to provide you with a quick resource you can use as a reference and save your time. But it will work for you only if you have read the book at least once. Here are the key ideas from this book.

A trucking company is an excellent business to start at present for several reasons. The trucking industry plays a significant role in moving goods throughout America. Up to around 72% of freight moves by road. A combination of the driver shortage, high freight demand, and increasing load prices is creating a demand for truck capacity. This presents an ideal opportunity to start a truck business. Furthermore, experts foresee the industry growing by a healthy 27% in the next decade. This offers a chance for business growth and an opportunity to grow your income as an owner.

Never start a trucking business without the right foundation and knowledge. It may be hard to start a trucking company, but the rewards are worth it. If you run your company well, you could profit around 7% of the business revenue. As you become more knowledgeable, skilled, and experienced, you could see your income swell to $100,000 or more per year. But even as a beginner, making income in the vicinity of $35,000 a year is not unheard of.

Part of running a successful trucking business involves creating a sound business plan. This working document forces you to think through the whole business startup process. Importantly, it guides your every move as you grow the business. That way, you may overcome mistakes that 85% of start-up trucking businesses make and fail.

If you want to run a legal business, you should register it with the government. You can choose your type of business entity between a sole proprietor, partnership, and limited liability company (LLC). I recommend organizing an LLC because you keep your personal and business assets separate. This is an excellent way to protect yourself or your business in the vent of a lawsuit.

The next vital legal aspect of a trucking business start-up is to get all the necessary licenses and permits. These will help you comply with various federal, state, or local laws. That way, you can operate your business with peace of mind. The key registration you must do is with the FMCSA to ensure you comply with trucking safety rules. And to obtain an operating authority so you can be paid for hauling freight. Don't forget to register for the necessary taxes, such as income, IFTA fuel, and sales tax. Remember that not all states charge income tax or gross receipts tax. Importantly, ensure you buy business insurance to cover liabilities in case events beyond your control occur.

It's impractical to try to run a trucking business without the right kind of vehicles. You can obtain these trucks by buying them outright or leasing them. And you can choose to either get new or used trucks. The key, though, is to ensure you purchase or lease mechanically sound vehicles. If you choose to lease, ensure that you select the right type. However, buying advantages you on the tax front. To make an informed decision, do a financial analysis of both leasing and buying.

If you choose to buy trucks, there are funding options available such as commercial truck financing, SBA loans. This is where your business plan and track record becomes vital. So, make sure that you have them.

Trucking is about moving loads from their sources to their destinations. Hence, you need to have drivers to operate the trucks. Even if you are an owner-operator, you still need to hire at least one driver to swap time off. So, having an ineffective recruitment strategy will go a long way to helping you hire the right kind of drivers. At the center of your truck driver hiring process should be finding employees with impeccable safety records.

Most importantly, it's vital to know how to find customers. They're the lifeblood of your business. Many strategies are available, including online marketing and personal prospecting. Running a business calls for negotiating skills. They'll help you win better-paying loads.

Finally, a business cannot succeed without sound financial management. You need to know the meaning of accounting terms like assets, liabilities, the cash flow statement, and the income statement. It is this accounting knowledge that's helpful when you analyze the profitability of your business. Most importantly, you need to manage the cash flow of your business. That's why you should have a cash-collection strategy.

I'm sure the knowledge and ideas you gained in this book will excite you to start your trucking business. There's no better time to become your own boss than now. Don't only read the book and let the knowledge sit in your mind without benefiting you and your loved ones. Go out there and apply what you've learned.

In conclusion, if you've found this book invaluable to your business knowledge, I would highly appreciate it if you could leave a glowing review.

References

Akalp, N. (2015, April 2). *How much does it cost to incorporate in each state?* Small Business Trends. https://smallbiztrends.com/2015/04/much-cost-incorporate-state.html

American Petroleum Institute. (2020, July). *Diesel tax.* www.Api.org. https://www.api.org/oil-and-natural-gas/consumer-information/motor-fuel-taxes/diesel-tax

American Trucking Associations. (n.d.). *Economics and industry data.* American Trucking Associations. https://www.trucking.org/economics-and-industry-data

Boyers, B. (2020, January 6). *How to apply for IFTA license and decals.* KeepTruckin. https://keeptruckin.com/blog/how-to-apply-ifta-license-decals

CDL.com. (n.d.). *How to start a trucking company [Your go-to guide].* CDL.com. https://www.cdl.com/trucking-resources/experienced-truck-drivers/how-to-start-trucking-company

Commercial Carrier Journal. (2019, October). *New research shows top reasons drivers leave within 90 days.* Commercial Carrier Journal. https://www.ccjdigital.com/new-research-shows-top-reasons-for-driver-turnover-within-90-days/

Corporation Service Company. (n.d.). *Start a trucking company in eight steps.* Corporation Service Company.

https://www.incorporate.com/learning-center/start-trucking-company-eight-steps/

Dalloo, C. (2019, December 18). *Eliminating deadhead miles in trucking.* DriverSource. https://www.driversource.net/2019/12/18/eliminating-deadhead-miles-in-trucking/

Della Rosa, J. (2020, September 29). *Trucking industry strength has 'staying power,' might last years, reports show.* Talk Business & Politics. https://talkbusiness.net/2020/09/trucking-industry-strength-has-staying-power-might-last-years-reports-show/

DOT Federal Highway Administration. (2020, June 23). *What is the HVUT and who must pay it?* Department of Transport Federal Highway Administration. https://www.fhwa.dot.gov/policyinformation/hvut/mod1/whatishvut.cfm

Driving Tests. (2020, June 13). *How to get a Commercial Driver License in 2020.* Driving Tests. https://driving-tests.org/how-to-get-a-cdl-license/

Federal Motor Carrier Safety Administration. (2019, December 16). *Insurance filing requirements.* Federal Motor Carrier Safety Administration. https://www.fmcsa.dot.gov/registration/insurance-filing-requirements

Federal Motor Carrier Safety Administration (FMCSA). (n.d.). *Applying for USDOT number and operating authority.* Federal Motor Carrier Safety Administration.

https://www.fmcsa.dot.gov/faq/applying-usdot-number-and-operating-authority

Freightos. (n.d.). *The beginner's guide to trucking: LTL Vs. FTL And other key trucking concepts.* Freightos. https://www.freightos.com/freight-resources/the-beginners-guide-to-trucking-ltl-vs-ftl-and-other-key-trucking-concepts/

Getloaded. (n.d.). *Starting a trucking company.* Www.Getloaded.com. http://www.getloaded.com/get-authority/how-to-start-a-trucking-business

John, S. (2019, June 3). *11 incredible facts about the $700 billion U.S. trucking industry.* Business Insider; Business Insider. https://markets.businessinsider.com/news/stocks/trucking-industry-facts-us-truckers-2019-5-1028248577

Motorcarrier HQ. (2019, November 11). *Understanding the UCR process and fees.* Motorcarrier HQ. https://www.motorcarrierhq.com/2015/07/14/understanding-the-ucr-process-and-fees/

Murray, J. (2020, May 22). *How can I get a Qualified Business Income deduction?* The Balance Small Business. https://www.thebalancesmb.com/how-can-i-get-a-qualified-business-income-deduction-4690835

PAM Transport. (n.d.). *Why we have one of the best truck lease purchase programs.* PAM Transport. https://pamdrivingjobs.com/why-we-have-one-of-the-best-truck-lease-purchase-programs/

Payne, R. (2016, February 3). *Empty trucks increase accident risk.* Phys.org; Science X Network. https://phys.org/news/2016-02-trucks-accident.html

PENSKE. (n.d.). *Lease vs buy a truck.* PENSKE. https://www.pensketruckleasing.com/full-service-leasing/leasing-benefits/lease-vs-own/

Randall-Reilly, & Commercial Carrier Journal. (2019). *What Drivers Want II.* Randall-Reilly. https://www.ccjdigital.com/wp-content/uploads/sites/10/2019/12/CCJ-What-Drivers-Want-Report-2019-2020-2019-12-04-10-14.pdf

Raphelson, S. (2018, January 9). *Trucking industry struggles with growing driver shortage.* NPR. https://www.npr.org/2018/01/09/576752327/trucking-industry-struggles-with-growing-driver-shortage

Resnick, R. (n.d.). *Setting up your business to receive payments.* Entrepreneur. https://www.entrepreneur.com/article/64838

Roadmaster Drivers School. (n.d.). *How much money do truck drivers make?* Roadmaster Drivers School. https://www.roadmaster.com/how-much-money-do-truck-drivers-make/

Rodela, J. (2018, October 23). *How much does it cost to start your trucking business?* KeepTruckin. https://keeptruckin.com/blog/cost-starting-trucking-business

Scott, A. (2018, October 27). *10 steps to setting up a limited liability company (LLC)*. The Balance Small Business. https://www.thebalancesmb.com/how-to-set-up-a-limited-liability-company-llc-1200859

STANDARD CARRIER ALPHA CODE (SCAC) APPLICATION. (n.d.). https://emanifestcentre.com/wp-core/wp-content/uploads/2010/06/SCAC-APPLICATION2.pdf

Trucking Job Finder. (n.d.). *Trucking laws and regulations*. Trucking Job Finder. https://www.truckingjobfinder.com/members/info/trucking-laws/